Marriage, Bible, Violence

Drawing on both biblical studies scholarship and practitioner experience, this book explores the disjuncture between complementarian accounts of biblical marriage and intersections of marriage and violence in texts from Jewish and Christian Scriptures.

This volume challenges authoritative complementarian claims to the Bible's allegedly clear and unequivocal directions on marriage. It refutes these claims with analysis of the muddled and often violent depictions of marriage in the Bible itself. Regular reminders show why such an exploration matters: that is, because recourse to the authority and 'plain meaning' of the Bible has had and continues to have impact on real people's lives. Sometimes, this impact is violent and traumatic, notably when the Bible is weaponised to justify intimate partner violence. This book explores a wide range of biblical texts and interpretations. Particular focus is placed on the influential pronouncements on 'biblical marriage' by the US Family Research Council and Council for Biblical Manhood and Womanhood. Textual analysis includes close focus on Genesis 1–3, Malachi 2, and Ephesians 5.

This book will appeal to students of biblical studies and theology, as well as anyone interested in research-based activism and in how sacred texts are directed towards modern day-to-day life. It investigates 'marriage', 'the Bible', and 'violence', all of which play significant roles in public discourses and popular culture.

Saima Afzal worked in local government, child protection, and as National Crime Agency-registered expert witness, Independent Member of the Lancashire (UK) Police Authority, with a national Equality, Diversity, and Human Rights portfolio. She has served as Assistant Police and Crime Commissioner and founded S.A.S. RIGHTS.

Johanna Stiebert is the Professor of Hebrew Bible at the University of Leeds (UK). She is author of *Rape Myths, the Bible and #MeToo* (Routledge, 2020) and has research interests in topics of gender, sexuality, and activism. She co-founded and co-directs The Shiloh Project (https://www.shilohproject.blog/).

Rape Culture, Religion and the Bible
Series Editors:
Emily Colgan, *Trinity Methodist Theological College, New Zealand*
Johanna Stiebert, *University of Leeds, UK*
Barbara Thiede, *University of North Carolina at Charlotte, USA*

The Bible and Sexual Violence Against Men
Chris Greenough

Rape Culture, Purity Culture, and Coercive Control in Teen Girl Bibles
Caroline Blyth

Trafficking Hadassah
Collective Trauma, Cultural Memory, and Identity in the Book of Esther and in the African Diaspora
Ericka Shawndricka Dunbar

Vocation and Violence
The Church and #MeToo
Miryam Clough

Zeus Syndrome
A Very Short History of Religion-Based Masculine Domination
Joachim Kügler

The Crucifixion of Jesus
Torture, Sexual Abuse, and the Scandal of the Cross
David Tombs

Marriage, Bible, Violence
Intersections and Impacts
Saima Afzal and Johanna Stiebert

For more information about this series, please visit: https://www.routledge.com/Rape-Culture-Religion-and-the-Bible/book-series/RCRB

Marriage, Bible, Violence
Intersections and Impacts

Saima Afzal and Johanna Stiebert

LONDON AND NEW YORK

First published 2024
by Routledge
4 Park Square, Milton Park, Abingdon, Oxon OX14 4RN

and by Routledge
605 Third Avenue, New York, NY 10158

Routledge is an imprint of the Taylor & Francis Group, an informa business

© 2024 Saima Afzal and Johanna Stiebert

The right of Saima Afzal and Johanna Stiebert to be identified as authors of this work has been asserted in accordance with sections 77 and 78 of the Copyright, Designs and Patents Act 1988.

All rights reserved. No part of this book may be reprinted or reproduced or utilised in any form or by any electronic, mechanical, or other means, now known or hereafter invented, including photocopying and recording, or in any information storage or retrieval system, without permission in writing from the publishers.

Trademark notice: Product or corporate names may be trademarks or registered trademarks, and are used only for identification and explanation without intent to infringe.

British Library Cataloguing-in-Publication Data
A catalogue record for this book is available from the British Library

ISBN: 978-0-367-71572-4 (hbk)
ISBN: 978-0-367-71573-1 (pbk)
ISBN: 978-1-003-15266-8 (ebk)

DOI: 10.4324/9781003152668

Typeset in Times New Roman
by KnowledgeWorks Global Ltd.

We dedicate this book to our mothers, Shamim Akhtar and Jan Stiebert, who led the way and not only gave us a voice but also amplified it.

Contents

Acknowledgements   *viii*

Introduction   1

Preliminaries 1
Marriage 4
The Bible 4
Violence 7
Bible, Marriage, and the Present 7

1 Biblical Marriage   12

2 Marriage in the Bible   36

Fixity 36
Marriage in the Bible: A Mixed Picture 40
Positive Depictions – With Some Caveats 41
Negative Depictions 45
Genesis 1–3 53
Ephesians 5:21–33 55
Malachi 2 56

3 Marriage, Bible, and Violence: Concluding Comments   66

Works Cited   *74*
Index of Biblical References   *84*
Index of Authors and Subjects   *87*

Acknowledgements

We would like to thank our wonderful editors, Emily Colgan and Barbara Thiede, who gave us so much encouragement and very prompt and constructive feedback. They also taught us more about Prophet Miriam, Ananias, and Sapphira. All errors and omissions that remain are on us.

The beginnings of this book predate the Covid pandemic, which changed our lives and those of everyone around us so dramatically, upending many plans, and causing delays with research and writing. Our perspectives and focus changed abruptly and sharply. Very many in our communities succumbed to the virus; some died. For our women-led Community Interest Company S.A.S. RIGHTS (www.sasrights.org), which Saima founded and we both co-direct, together with Mmapula Kebaneilwe and Emma Tomalin, things suddenly took off.

S.A.S. RIGHTS serves vulnerable members in our local communities who need help navigating healthcare provision, social, legal, and safeguarding services – often in desperate circumstances. Consequently, S.A.S. RIGHTS became a front-row seat for seeing the statistics of accelerating domestic violence and abuse during the pandemic lived out.

Saima quickly formed a virtual team around us, and we got busy running online well-being and exercise workshops and counselling sessions, creating and disseminating infographics, organising collections of food and furniture, fundraising, and assembling activists from all over the world for International Women's Day and the Sixteen Days of Activism.

The harder it was to find time for writing, the clearer the importance of this book became for us. We could see the harm and damage caused by instrumentalising sacred texts to afflict real people, with women and girls disproportionately represented among victims and survivors. Resisting this on multiple fronts, including with research-based arguments, drove us on.

This book is a collaboration between us. Each of us identifies as both scholar and activist, even if in our working lives, these carry different emphases. We share a conviction that activism benefits from a basis in research and research benefits from having impact on positive social change.

Introduction

Preliminaries

This book aims to interrogate, evaluate, and sometimes challenge what is commonly asserted and accepted about 'biblical marriage' – especially when assertions are made from a place of authority, and when they exert discriminatory or otherwise damaging impact on real people. It seeks to demonstrate first, that the very practice of giving normativity to ancient written texts and, by extension, to those who claim authority to interpret these, can do harm. This applies not only to the Bible – used as the example text for this book – but also to other religious canons. Moreover, it shows that this practice is very much one of proof-texting, that is, of selecting those texts that support a predetermined agenda, while playing down, or downright ignoring, other texts that also have something to say on the topic but do not fit the agenda.

Our focus is biblical texts, because study of the Bible is Johanna's area of expertise and, more importantly, because the Bible is enormously and widely influential, including in the authors' own UK location. No other text is as widely translated, published, and disseminated as the Bible, which is the biggest bestseller of all time, as well as in each and every year. But the Bible is not alone in being accorded canonicity or to be invoked for inculcating prescriptions regarding marriage. Saima has experienced violence that was sanctioned by clerics and community leaders who made recourse to Islamic sacred texts. She has also, as a practitioner and activist, worked with members from a range of faith communities (Christian, Muslim, Hindu, and Sikh) and is aware of sacred texts from each of these traditions being drawn on to legitimate human rights violations.[1] While other religious texts and traditions cannot be considered here more than fleetingly, some of the explorations of this book will have bearing and relevance beyond the faiths and traditions associated with the Bible.[2]

This book is not about 'dissing' either marriage or the Bible. We do not dispute that marriage, including marriage founded on religious ideals and foundations, can be fulfilling and sustaining. Nor do we dispute that there may well have been happy marital unions also in those distant ages vaguely designated 'biblical times'.[3] But we do intend to probe how well what is sometimes labelled 'biblical marriage' stacks up against 'what the Bible says about marriage'. We do not make any claims to offering the 'true' or 'right' interpretation of biblical marriage. In fact, we resist the idea that there even is such a thing. Even if there were, moreover, we would, in the event of the interpretation being harmful, advocate rejecting it. Instead, we want to point out how such authoritative claims can be damaging, particularly when they convey ideologies that either discriminate against those excluded from 'biblical marriage',[4] or consign those suffering within a marriage to remaining married, without recourse to divorce.

There indeed exist interpretations of biblical passages on marriage that propel agendas we find appealing. *Living in Love & Faith* (LLF)[5] points to interpretations arguing 'that the Bible's view on marriage can legitimately include same-sex couples', because marriage, as depicted in Scripture, celebrates above all 'loving faithfulness and covenant loyalty'[6] rather than the sexes of married persons (LLF 2020: 282). And Helen Paynter in her book confidently titled *The Bible Doesn't Tell Me So* (2020), debunks as 'myths'[7] the notion that the Bible in any way condones domestic abuse or coercive control in marriage. Instead, Paynter reads the Bible as a text that first, speaks to and defends the oppressed and victimised, and second, through the model of Jesus, promotes non-toxic and nurturing masculinity and relationships. We *much* prefer Paynter's healing and constructive model, both to the justifications of violence in some prophetic metaphors describing marriage in crisis, which have been exposed in their full brutality and misogyny by Renita Weems (1995), and to Andreas Köstenberger's exclusionary delineation of biblical marriage (to be explored shortly). We applaud the positive action liberatory interpretations such as Paynter's can inspire, but we are still unwilling to designate them as definitively 'true' or 'correct'.

Neither author of this book has a stake in the Bible – in the sense that either regards the Bible as a text determinative or normative for their actions, values, beliefs, or behaviours. This is not to be confused with claiming objectivity in interpreting the Bible. Both authors are mindful of how positionality shapes the interpretive process and own up to a subjective standpoint. Both authors identify as feminist[8] and cishet[9] and come together to examine biblical marriage from distinct perspectives. Saima is British Pakistani and holds a Master of Religious Studies and Public Life. She was coerced into and escaped from what is sometimes called a 'forced marriage'. Saima resists the designation when applied to her because she never consented: consequently, she denies any validity – legal, civic, or religious – to her so-called 'marriage'. Saima is now a community organiser, consultant, and activist whose work focuses particularly on domestic violence and 'honour' crimes. She has worked principally in Lancashire and Yorkshire, and also elsewhere in the UK, in culturally diverse communities. Johanna is a scholar of Hebrew language and Bible, interested in how the Bible functions in present-day settings, with particular focus on gender-based violence. She is co-founder of the Shiloh Project, which explores rape culture, religion, and the Bible. She is married and acknowledges the privileges and social capital this confers. Both authors are interested in how religion 'works' and influences in the present and both share a commitment to advancing human rights and social justice. Both are co-directors of S.A.S. RIGHTS, a community interest group founded by Saima.[10]

Returning briefly to the matter of objectivity, alluded to above: we cannot and do not claim objectivity. This is first, because we doubt an objective or dispassionate approach to the Bible is possible for us, and second, because we see merit in subjectivity. In a book that is focused on violence in and about marriage, the research of, for instance, a scholar with no first-hand experience of forced or otherwise abusive marriage, could certainly have something worthwhile to contribute and such a scholar may indeed have a good case to make in terms of their objectivity on the topic – but a strong case can also be made for the subjective perspective and scholarship of Saima, who *has* experience of forced and abusive marriage. We also hold that there are topics on which recourse to 'objectivity' and its ostensible claims to balance and dispassion is wrongheaded. When it comes to racism, sexism, homophobia, transphobia, and other such kinds of profoundly harmful discriminations and prejudices, we do not call for 'balance' or 'counter arguments' – we call, and we should call it out for what it is: *wrong*. As will emerge, because we do not feel bound by the Bible or assert it to be in its entirety the word of God and truth for all time, we feel free to call some of what the Bible says about marriage wrong and as contributing to or covering up rape cultures.[11]

We want to make a scholarly contribution, and we also want to be mindful of biblical texts and their interpretations existing in spaces where both violence in marriage and spiritual abuse are real and commonplace.[12] Scholarship on marriage, the Bible, and violence, we believe, needs to consider its potential resonances and impacts and to acknowledge the pain it can bring. We admire and draw from the recent work of feminist scholars such as Nancy Tan and Frances Klopper, among others, who precede us. Hence, Klopper (2021) engages critical empathy to read Psalm 55 in the light of rape trauma, while Tan (2021) shows how biblical passages referring to 'prostitutes' are received and cause pain and harm to actual sex workers. Both scholars are performing activism by embedding reminders of and reflections on lived traumatic experiences in their academic writing. Such reminders function as 'wake-up calls' to action. We hope to offer something similar, including with the short interjecting passages in the two chapters to follow, which refer directly to Saima's practitioner work.

This book is a co-production. We each bring different experiences, backgrounds, and skill-sets, and we have worked together throughout to combine these. We are inspired by the collaborations between academic and non-academic individuals and communities in South Africa and Botswana, including those of our mutual friend, womanist biblical scholar, activist, and S.A.S. RIGHTS co-director Mmapula Kebaneilwe. Central to such collaborations is – in the words of South African scholar of religion Gerald West – 'refusal to be "dispassionate" [and a] commitment to creativity and "engagement"' (West 2019: 23). Like West and Kebaneilwe, we, too, advocate that interpretation of the Bible demands 'actual engagement with the gendered realities of life' as well as the endeavour to confront gendered and other injustices (West 2019: 23).

Marriage

Marriage, when conceptualised broadly, is a cultural institution establishing rights and obligations between (normally) two persons and – very often – also between them and other kin (both consanguines, such as lineal ascendants or descendants, and affines, such as parents-in-law). Marriage appears widely in lists of human common denominators. (The pursuit of human, or cultural universals that transpired in such lists, was popular in the earlier twentieth century among social scientists. Alongside this universality of marriage, however, its cultural variability and diversity are also acknowledged.[13]) Some generalisations do apply: hence, most marriages involve sanctions or rights to do with sexual access. Quite often, for instance, a marriage rite, such as a betrothal, or a wedding ceremony, is recommended, or even prescribed, prior to sexual contact between persons; in some settings, marriage presumes or grants blanket consent to sexual access.[14] But much of the detail of marriage – including who can marry whom (which may be circumscribed by age, gender, caste, relatedness,[15] status, religion, family approval, and other factors) – or the ceremony conferring marriage (commonly called a 'wedding') are acutely variable from culture to culture and through time.[16]

Important to mention, too, is that for all its ubiquity, marriage is in all sorts of ways an exclusionary institution, tied up in complicated ways with such matters as convention, tradition, citizenship, belonging, and cultural acceptance. As Leigh Moscowitz points out, because marriage is defined in particular ways, it 'legitimizes some individuals and relationships by prohibiting others' (Moscowitz 2013: 5). Furthermore, marriage regulations as part of larger hegemonic power structures have imposed on marginal groups and on '[c]onstructions of gendered, raced, classed, and sexual identities' and ensured 'an overall set of power relations that privilege reproduction and heterosexuality' (Moscowitz 2013: 12).

The Bible

'The Bible' means different things to different groups of people and is made up of a concatenation of ancient texts that hold canonical status for Jews and Christians. In Judaism, 'the Bible' is also called 'Tanakh'. Christians call a closely related set of texts 'the Old Testament'. Scholars often refer to the texts Jewish tradition relies on as 'the Hebrew Bible' but *The Jewish Study*

Bible deems the term 'a redundancy', because 'Jews have no other Bible but the "Hebrew Bible"' (Berlin and Brettler 2004: x). For Christians, 'the Bible' includes also the books collectively called 'the New Testament', or, 'the Greek Bible', and sometimes additional books as well.[17]

For the purposes of this book, 'the Bible' refers to the books of either the Hebrew or Greek Bibles – that is, to the canon of the Jewish community and/or to the books held sacred in common by Christians. One reason for extending the focus beyond Johanna's primary academic expertise in the area of Jewish texts, is to avoid the common supersessionist impression that any problem with 'the Bible' lies with the Jewish 'old' covenant, while the 'new' Christian covenant inaugurates peace and love.[18] When it comes to the topic of marriage (and this is not a singular example) what 'the Bible' says is both mixed and (at least potentially) problematic in *each* of Jewish and Christian sacred literatures. Given the inclusion of Greek Bible texts in this book, that is, of texts which hold *no* canonical value in Jewish communities, Christian interpretation and application predominate here.[19] We concede also that 'to pretend that a particular canon is normative simply because it is accepted by a majority ... is to be complicit in ... an ideology of normalization. ...To simply discount a different canon solely on the basis that it is less popular – at this particular time – would be to fail to acknowledge [both Judaism's and] Christianity's own history' (Tong 2022). At the same time, we need to impose some boundaries.

It certainly matters to us that the texts of the Hebrew Bible are acknowledged as in the first instance Jewish texts. Moreover, we advocate for close and critical scrutiny of Christian interpretation and usage of biblical texts – both to disclose supersessionist tendencies that, wittingly or not, contribute to Judeophobia,[20] and because these interpretations and usages often wield considerable power. Christianity has the most followers of any world religion, with around 2.2 billion followers (or more than 31% of the world population). Indeed, there are almost as many Southern Baptists (13,680,493) as Jews (estimated 15 million). For all the antisemitic claims of Jewish power, control, and designs on world dominion, which have by no means evaporated along with the exposure of The Protocols of the Elders of Zion as calumny over a century ago (Eisner 2006), it is certain Christian lobbies that have far greater reach, influence, power, and, therewith, scope for causing harm. This explains our focus (in Chapter 1) on Christian interpretation and also our inclusion of interrogation of some Greek Bible passages.

That 'the Bible' is an authoritative or canonical text is widely asserted but deserves some pause and qualification. First, there is no 'original' text of either Hebrew or Greek Bible. Referring to '*an* ancient' text (rather than *the* ancient text) is the best we can do. Any biblical text is a copy of copies, bearing signs of complex textual development and redaction. Both Hebrew and Greek Bibles are compiled of a diverse collection of texts spanning – in the case of the Hebrew Bible in particular – a large expanse of time. Indeed, the Hebrew

Bible evidences a range of Hebrew languages, or, at the very least, evidence of considerable diachronic development of Biblical Hebrew, as well as passages in another Semitic language, namely Aramaic.[21] Whereas the Hebrew Bible tends to use one ancient text as its copy text – namely the Masoretic Text represented by the Leningrad Codex, the oldest complete manuscript of the Hebrew Bible – the Greek Bible has been compiled from a selection of documents using the criteria of textual criticism to determine (in the case of multiple versions) the preferable version of several, or many.

These backstage processes complicate the quest for understanding what (the) text 'says' and 'means'. Translations do not resolve complexities and are themselves processes of interpretation (and sometimes guesswork) and conveyers of ideology. To give one example, relevant to the topic of marriage, the single Hebrew word *ishshâ* is variously translated in English bibles as either 'woman' or 'wife'. Translators decide which of the two they deem more appropriate, relying predominantly on literary context. This is entirely appropriate; in English the meaning of 'fall', too, for example, is decided depending on context. It is context that makes clear whether 'fall' is used as a noun or verb, or whether it is a synonym for dropping, or becoming lower, or for autumn. (Context also determines whether 'lab' is short for 'laboratory' or 'Labrador'.) But translation is also swayed by ideology. Hence, Ken Stone points out that the translation of *'eshet lapîdôt* (Judg 4:4) as '*wife* of Lappidoth', rather than a second legitimate rendering, '*woman* of torches' (or 'fiery woman'), provides Deborah with a spouse where none is otherwise indicated (Stone 2015: 174–175). Arguably, the alternative translation confers power and fierceness, which aligns well with Deborah's status as prophet, judge, and military leader (Judg 4:4, 9–10). Then again, maybe (whether this is unconscious or strategic), the singularity, even radicality, of a female judge may have disturbed translators to the point of wanting to make her more conventional and respectable, and hence, to locate her within familiar kinship structures, thereby making her a wife (albeit of an otherwise unknown man with an unusual name).[22]

To give another example, this time from the Greek Bible (and again focusing on an expression relevant to the topic at issue), translation is particularly tricky when encountering euphemism. The admonition at 1 Thessalonians 4:4 is to possess one's own 'vessel' in holiness and honour. This is in a wider context of condemning sexual impropriety. What is disputed (as evidenced in various translations) is whether this 'vessel' refers to possessing, perhaps controlling, one's own sexual member, or one's body (NRSV), or whether this is a euphemism for acquiring a wife of one's own (D'Angelo 2014: 497).

Different persons and communities commit to different translations of 'the Bible' – sometimes for ideological considerations. In Anglophone contexts, the most widely used translation in Jewish communities is that of JPS (Jewish Publication Society). In many academic contexts, the regularly used version is NRSV (New Revised Standard Version)[23] or NRSVUE (NRSV Updated

Edition). Many devotional communities prefer either NIV (New International Version), or KJV (King James Version). Others claim that NASV (New American Standard Version) is closest to Hebrew and Greek versions. Such choices, dissents, and justifications for different translations, are often ideologically guided but completely obscured in confident or prescriptive claims of what 'the text says' and what 'the text means'.[24]

Violence

For the purposes of this book, we take 'violence' to pertain to the World Health Organisation's broad definition of 'intentional use of physical force, or power, threatened or actual' that 'either results in or has a high likelihood of resulting in injury, death, psychological harm, maldevelopment, or deprivation' (WHO). We emphasise particularly gendered violence and the relationships between power and violence, which transpire in a tendency for those with most power (i.e., hegemonic males) to be able to exert most violence.[25] This, in turn, has particularly deleterious consequences for women and girls.

We argue and will illustrate that there is a frequent association between gendered violence and marriage in the Bible. Moreover, the Bible and its interpretations are used to facilitate or justify real-life violence. We have tried – often in endnotes – to give some sense of the manifold manifestations of such violence. Yes, this violence can and does take the form of physical abuse (e.g., domestic battery, femicide), but it can also cause violence by other means (e.g., coercive control), and through what it promotes (e.g., procreation, or purity culture, or rape culture), condemns (e.g., divorce, same-sex loving, consensual polyamory), or silences (e.g., counter-interpretations of biblical text, alternative sources of authority, development of knowledge and understanding since 'biblical times', or speaking up against empowered interpreters or leaders).

Bible, Marriage, and the Present

'The Bible' is also considered significant, or interesting for reasons other than canonicity, such as on account of its historical influence on iconography, laws, or literature, for instance, and because of its abiding presence and impact in not just faith communities, but also political, artistic, popular culture, and digital contexts.[26] Moreover, faith communities, while arguably the primary audience of biblical texts, intersect with other spheres of influence, such as, to give one example, the political arena.[27] Alongside these many tributaries of influence from the Bible, marriage, too, continues to be very much in the fore of public debates. Also, while in many Western democracies, the marriage rate may be steadily decreasing, particularly among opposite-sex couples (e.g., for the UK, see ONS 2020 and LLF 2020: 68–69), the prominence of marriage and weddings in popular culture is striking and unabating.[28]

Sometimes 'Bible' and 'marriage' come together very prominently. One example is the debates around clerical marriage in those Christian denominations that have historically drawn on the apparent celibacy of both Jesus and Paul the Apostle to prohibit priests from marrying.[29] But by far most coverage and international reach has in these first decades of the twenty-first century fixated on same-sex marriage, or marriage equality,[30] with religious conservatives, including Christians who draw on the Bible, counting among its most prominent and fervent opponents.[31] If, whether, where, and when persons of the same sex can marry, even if 'marriage' can be used to signify a same-sex union,[32] can legitimately be designated an *idée fixe* of our times. Mark Gevisser (2020), evocatively, speaks of a 'Pink Line' that has created alliances and divisions on a global scale. Leigh Moscowitz, meanwhile, albeit writing prior to the Supreme Court overturning of Roe v Wade in 2022, refers to same-sex marriage in the USA context as the 'central battle waged in the culture wars', replacing abortion as 'the most volatile social issue' (Moscowitz 2013: 2–3). It has also been the focus of deep divisions in religious communities.[33] Given the preoccupation with and public prominence of both the Bible and marriage, right up to the present, as well as their entanglements, it becomes compelling to examine biblical marriage.

Notes

1 Saima has worked for many years in the areas of local government, child protection, honour-based crime, and forced marriage, as a National Crime Agency-registered expert witness, an independent member of the Lancashire Police Authority, with a national Equality, Diversity, and Human Rights portfolio. She has served as an Assistant Police and Crime Commissioner in Lancashire and within her own organisation S.A.S. RIGHTS.

2 There is a growing literature on the complicity of religious actors and factors in gender-based and sexual violence, including in the context of intimate relationships and marriage. On domestic abuse in multiple religious settings and traditions (Christian, Jewish, Muslim, Buddhist, Hindu, Sikh, and some minority movements), see Johnson (2015). On sexual violence legitimated by a range of sacred texts (Jewish, Christian, and Islamic), see Kalmanofsky (2017). On the intersections of religion and rape culture (though predominantly focused on the Bible and Christian contexts), see the three volumes edited by Blyth, Colgan, and Edwards (2018). On abuse in Christian marriage worldwide, see Koepping (2022, *passim*), and also her appendix on Buddhist and Muslim contexts (2022: 157–166). For abuse in Buddhist communities and on the notion of 'consent' in Buddhist scriptures, see Langenberg and Gleig (2020).

3 While some authors have something quite concise in mind when they say 'biblical times' – e.g., Ebeling, for whom this pertains to Iron Age I Israel c.1200–1000 BCE (Ebeling 2010 *passim*) – the time periods depicted *in the Bible*, or even the time spans *over which the constituent texts of the Bible were written,* cover multiple centuries.

4 This applies to those who love and desire to marry someone of the same, rather than another, sex, and those in fulfilling polyamorous relationships. At the time of writing, a captivating book by Kahn-Harris, interpreting the Naomi-Ruth-Boaz triad in the book of Ruth as a successful polyamorous marriage is in production.

5 On LLF, see below.
6 We will problematise the notion that marriage in the Bible is consistently so positive and probe the connection between marriage and covenant (see below).
7 See the back cover of Paynter's book. The word 'myth' is potentially confusing because it has two discrete meanings: either 'a traditional story', or 'a widely held but false belief' (see Stiebert 2020: 61). The latter meaning is intended here.
8 Chaudhry makes clear that feminism is not univocal and can clash in a variety of ways with the groups she calls patriarchal coreligionists and cultural relativist liberals. In Chaudhry's terms, Saima better fits the label of 'religious feminist', who seeks 'to identify methods of interpretation that could engender a process of healing from sexual violence and abuse perpetrated in and through sacred scripture'. Johanna inclines more to what Chaudhry calls a supersessionist feminist, in the sense that this group constructs religion as 'irredeemably patriarchal' (Chaudhry 2017: 95).
9 The vocabulary of gender and sexuality is nuanced and evolving. On the meanings of 'cis', 'straight', 'cishet' (i.e., cis + heterosexual) and other terms in this orbit, see the accessible explanations of Ferguson on healthline.com.
10 On the Shiloh Project, see https://shilohproject.blog/. For more about Saima, including why she is uncomfortable with the word 'honour' when used in relation to particular killings and other crimes, as well as on her model for addressing what she calls 'Community Coercion Control', see the extended interview with her (Stiebert 2018b).
11 On rape culture and the Bible, see Thiede (2022b: 3–11). That such covering up, including of serious crimes such as sexual harassment and rape, occurs in churches is documented in the writings of Christian insiders that combine the perspectives of subjective experience and biblical and theological scholarship (see, Brown 2009; Everhart 2020; Barr 2021; and Clough 2022).
12 For evidence on violence in marriage with specific reference to the UK, see ONS 2020. On spiritual abuse and gender-based violence, see Tomalin (2023).
13 A more recent examination, as well as critique, of cultural universality is by Brown (1991). Brown also discusses marriage at length.
14 Historically, coverture laws, which 'subsumed' women's rights into their husbands' upon marriage, were defended with recourse to the Bible and a wife and husband becoming 'one flesh' (Gen 2:24; Mt 19:5; Mk 10:8; Eph 5). In the UK, such laws lasted well into the nineteenth century and meant that wives' property became their husbands' and allowed husbands to control and decide over their wives, including their bodies. Rape in marriage was only acknowledged in UK law in 1991. Prior to this, it was commonly held that marriage conferred 'conjugal rights', with 'I do' eliminating the option of 'I don't want to'.
15 Incest is widely cited (e.g., Murdock 1945; Brown 1991) as another cultural universal. Incest refers to 'taboo sexual relations with anyone too closely related for marriage to be permissible' (Stiebert 2016: 1). This reaffirms the ubiquity of marriage, alongside the ubiquity of marriage taboos.
16 E.g., see Brown (1991, Kindle Locator 1733), summarising the debate as to whether 'marriage' can be meaningfully defined in all its cultural variability.
17 The canon of the Catholic and Eastern Christian Churches also includes the deuterocanonical books (called 'the Apocrypha' in Protestant contexts) and the Orthodox Tewahedo canon includes these, as well as additional books, too. We accept that 'Greek Bible' in some contexts pertains to the Jewish translation also called 'the Septuagint' (LXX), which includes the books contained in the Hebrew Bible and Apocrypha/deuterocanonical books. We apply 'Greek Bible' (in parallel with 'Hebrew Bible') to the books also called 'New Testament'.
18 For a discussion of supersessionism and antisemitism in Christian interpretation, see Reaves (2020). On violence in Christian texts, including the Greek Bible, see especially Matthews and Gibson (2005) and Cobb and Vanden Eykel (2022).

10 *Introduction*

19 Jewish interpretation has, however, since the emergence, growing distinctiveness, formalisation, and accelerating spread and widening dominance of Christianity, often developed in relationship and in opposition to Christian interpretation. While we do not like the merger term 'Judeo-Christian', there has existed extensive influence between the two, which has worked in multiple directions. For a full investigation, see Boyarin (2004). Consequently, while Jewish interpretation is certainly often distinctive, it is not immune to, or always entirely separable from, Christian interpretation. Much of what we discuss here has analogy or relevance also for traditions other than Christian ones.
20 For Christian supersessionist Judeophobia, see Rollens, Vanden Eykel, and Warren (2020).
21 See Sáenz-Badillo (1993).
22 Biblical women are often described in relational terms: i.e., as some male's daughter, wife, mother, or sister. There is no (other) relational term for Deborah. Unusually, while she *is* called a mother, she is not described as mother to sons, or daughters, but as 'mother in Israel' (Judg 5:7). Another case, like Stones's, for gendered distortion is made by Schäfer-Bossert (1994), who points out that the Hebrew word *'ôn* is translated 'strength' or 'vigour' when it pertains to men generating sons (e.g., Gen 49:3) but not when Rachel in childbirth names her son *ben-'ônî* (Gen 35:18). The latter is regularly translated 'son of my sorrow' (not, 'son of my strength').
23 We use the NRSV translation unless otherwise stated.
24 Brettler (2005), while he does not explore the full depth of the radical potential of biblical texts' messiness and variety, provides great insight into some of the reasons for the complexities of reading and interpreting the Hebrew Bible.
25 We do not deny or exclude the existence of other power dynamics. E.g., see note 15 in Chapter 1.
26 For a collection of essays demonstrating the Bible's influence on advertising, political rhetoric, street art, stand-up comedy, popular literature, and television, among others, see Edwards (2015). On the Bible, social media, and digital cultures, see Phillips (2020).
27 On the influence of ultra-orthodox parties Shas and United Torah Judaism in the Knesset's committees and cabinet, see Gur (2020). On the well-documented alliance between Christian evangelical movements and the Republican Party in the USA, see Fea et al (2018) and Du Mez (2020), as well as below. In the UK context, politicians' faith commitment is sometimes depicted as an impediment, rather than asset (e.g., Tim Farron quit as Liberal Democrat leader in 2017, citing that his Christian faith was incompatible with leading his party; and Kate Forbes's membership in the Free Church of Scotland drew significant attention, much of it negative, in the Scottish National Party leadership contest of 2023). The influence of the Church of England (CofE) is nonetheless prominent. The House of Commons has its own CofE chaplain and official spokesperson, the Second Church Estates Commissioner. The House of Lords has secured representation of the Archbishops of Canterbury and York alongside other senior CofE bishops. Both Houses open with Christian prayers.
28 Ongoing preoccupation with weddings and marriage is reflected in, for example, their prominence in popular television shows. All of *Married at First Sight* (Channel 4, advertised as 'Singletons, matched by a panel of experts, marry a total stranger who *[sic]* they meet for the very first time on their wedding day'), *Love is Blind* (Netflix, following couples who become engaged without setting eyes on each other and deciding at the altar whether to split or marry), *Wife Swap* (ABC, Paramount, since 2004, where two wives, usually from very different backgrounds, swap families for two weeks), *Say Yes To the Dress* (TLC, focused around the 'perfect' wedding dress) and *Don't Tell the Bride* (BBC, Sky, where grooms organise a wedding without input from their brides), among others, attest to this.

Introduction 11

29 Some Orthodox Christian denominations permit clerical marriage if it occurs prior to ordination. Catholicism, however, prescribes clerical celibacy.
30 The first legislation legalising same-sex marriage came into effect in 2001, in the Netherlands.
31 While African church leaders are often open to, or even openly defying, their church's teaching on clerical marriage (Perriello 2013), they are also, alongside clerics of Islamic states, the most virulently opposed to same-sex marriage (Gevisser 2020: 35–36). This was reaffirmed (regarding Anglican African church leaders) at the Lambeth Conference 2022 (Taduggoronno 2022). It is also a crass oversimplification, however, to depict the vast and richly diverse continent of Africa, or the manifold African Christianities, as only or rigorously homophobic (see van Klinken 2019).
32 At the time of writing, same-sex marriage is legal and recognised in 29 nation-states. These include nine from the Americas, sixteen from Europe, Australia, and New Zealand, but just one each from Africa (South Africa) and Asia (Taiwan). More than 30 nation-states have gendered constitutional definitions of 'marriage' that specify unions of a man and a woman, while nation-states with constitutionally mandated Islamic law, proscribe same-sex marriage.
33 Gevisser describes how 2013 saw both the UK passing the Marriage (Same Sex Couples) Act *and* Nigeria 'promulgat[ing] its antithesis: the Same Sex Marriage (Prohibition) Act … the harshest anti-homosexuality law in the world outside of Islamic Sharia' (Gevisser 2020: 12). Gevisser also explains that given the globalisation of both sexual and gender identities, on the one hand, and religious identity on the other, clashes became inevitable. He cites as one example the 'cultural bifurcation' in Malaysia, where conservative Islamism gained purchase in response to and in the face of demand for LGBT rights (Gevisser 2020: 15). The Netflix documentary *Pray Away,* directed by Stolakis (2021) illustrates the mobilisation of religious lobbies against what they characterised as the 'gay agenda'. While the documentary focuses most on the damage wrought by Christian so-called 'ex gay' organisations, it also reports on the polarisation around Proposition 8 in the California state elections. This proposition banning same sex marriage was passed in November 2008 and overturned shortly after.

1 Biblical Marriage

'Biblical marriage' refers for our purposes to a prominent Christian ideology about marriage. This ideology claims to represent what the Bible and God really 'say' on the topic, and to derive from this claim an authoritative blueprint for conduct; in particular, conduct concerning gendered relations, which are conceived of in complementarian, that is, strictly binary and heteronormative, terms. For all its decisive assertions, however, biblical marriage ideology is constructed in highly selective ways, with proof-texts chosen, interpreted, or ignored in accordance with agenda-driven criteria. 'Biblical marriage' is also distinct from at least some of the content about marriage in the Bible – the topic of Chapter 2.

We will turn next to two prominent sources that well represent conservative and, some would say, orthodox claims about biblical marriage. The first source is *Recovering Biblical Manhood & Womanhood* (RBMW 2006), a large volume with multiple contributions by members of the Council for Biblical Manhood and Womanhood (CBMW), whose mission is to describe and promote complementarianism: namely, 'the teachings of the Bible about the complementary differences between men and women, created equally in the image of God'. The authors' assertion is that lived complementarianism is 'essential for obedience to Scripture and for the health of the family and the church'.[1] The second source is Andreas J. Köstenberger's 'The Bible's Teaching on Marriage and Family', promoted by the Family Research Council (FRC), which describes itself as promoting a 'biblical worldview'.[2] Both publications share much common ground and are widely disseminated and available open access online. Both purport to represent biblical marriage, asserting that the Bible contains a clear blueprint.[3]

We will also refer, if more fleetingly, to the recent publication by the Archbishops' Council of the Church of England, *Living in Love & Faith* (LLF), which describes itself as the document of 'a learning journey', including on the Christian teaching and learning about marriage.[4] LLF, too, is grounded in the Bible, which is identified as the ultimate source of the Church's inspiration and authority (LLF 2020: 24). The literature of LLF is distinct from that of the CBMW and FRC in some interesting respects, but all have considerable international dissemination, reach, and influence.[5] While LLF is best characterised as (small 'c') 'conservative' rather than as typical of the right-wing UK Conservative (or Tory) Party,[6] CBMW and FRC are both associated with Right-wing elements of the US Republican Party. These associations are very easy to identify[7] and speak to a particular brand of ideological agenda, characterised by adamant opposition to all of elective abortion, feminism,[8] and, of course, LGBTQ+ identities, sexual expressions, and rights.[9] We are not denying that many others use the Bible to defend various and alternative ideologies (they do),[10] or that we have ideologies of our own (we do).[11] We are concerned here with describing and then problematising ideology in the sense of an agenda, or vested interest, claimed or passed off as biblically verified truth, and applied with a view to social control. This has as one consequence that such terms as 'human dignity' and 'religious liberty', for instance (used liberally on FRC), have a particular and narrow meaning that would not embrace the human dignity of transgender being, or the religious liberty of two Christian persons of the same sex to be married in church.[12] Feminism, moreover, is constructed not as polyvocal[13] or aimed at equality and human fulfilment, but as bent on destroying God's order and as amplifying a 'homosexual agenda'. Feminism, according to this ideology, lures women into 'secular employment' and, consequently, away from God's will, the home and family (Piper and Grudem 2006: 56). John Piper and Wayne Grudem argue in this vein that 'feminist minimization of sexual role differentiation contributes to the confusion of sexual identity that ... gives rise to more homosexuality in society' (Piper and Grudem 2006: 82). They go on (rather histrionically), to claim feminists' 'movement away from role distinctions grounded in the natural created order... [leads] inevitably to the overthrow of normative heterosexuality' (Piper and Grudem 2006: 83). This is stressed repeatedly and in alarmist terms: 'To us it is increasingly and painfully clear that Biblical feminism is an unwitting partner in unravelling the fabric of complementary manhood and womanhood that provides the foundation not only for Biblical marriage and Biblical church order, but also for heterosexuality itself' (Piper and Grudem 2006: 77).

In their argument, masculine males, and feminine females, each with clear and 'complementary' roles, properly join in heteronormative marriage, which is characterised as *both* natural and God-ordained. This leads on to their claim that, according to 'clinical evidence ... there is no such thing as a "homosexual child"' (Piper and Grudem 2006: 84).[14] In other words, homosexuality is designated unnatural, ungodly, and unbiblical, and as deriving from either deviant (such as feminist) upbringing or deviant choice. Abuse, too, like homosexuality, stems from feminism, certainly not from any 'biblical' values. Piper and Grudem consider the question whether male headship and female submission could result in domestic abuse (cf. Paynter 2020) but conclude that the answer is 'No'. This is above all because male headship is 'Christlike, sacrificial' and keeps 'the good of the wife in view and regards her as a joint heir of the grace of life (1 Peter 3:7)' (Piper and Grudem, RBMW 2006: 62). Instead, they make a counter-case, targeting feminism as the harm-doer:

> we believe that wife abuse (and husband abuse)[15] have some deep roots in the failure of parents to impart to their sons and daughters the meaning of true masculinity and true femininity. The confusions and frustrations of sexual identity often explode in harmful behaviors. The solution to this is not to minimize gender differences (which will then break out in menacing ways), but to teach in the home and the church how true manhood and womanhood express themselves in the loving and complementary roles of marriage.
>
> (Piper and Grudem, RBMW 2006: 62)

Again, *they* assert what constitutes 'true masculinity and true femininity' and decide it should be taught 'in the home and the church' to express 'true manhood and womanhood' in terms of the biblical 'complementary roles of marriage' *they* determine. Whereas some Bible-using and quoting Christians acknowledge that the Bible can be and has been used or abused to facilitate spousal abuse – most often of wives by husbands (Paynter 2020),[16] RBMW denies this and instead targets feminism as root cause.

While there are some nods in RBMW to humility, there is also smugness[17] and authors insist that they represent the content of 'the Bible' and, therefore, God's will.[18] Endorsements on the back cover of RBMW claim God is working through this book and that it is a 'faithful guide to understanding and applying the Bible's teaching on gender'. Piper uses 'according to the Bible' in his subtitle and explains this as bringing his chapter 'into *accord* with what the Bible teaches', by offering reflections that are 'not the creation of an independent mind, but the fruit of a tree planted firmly in the soil of constant meditation on the Word of God' (Piper, RBMW 2006: 32). Piper and Grudem assert that their convictions concerning biblical manhood, womanhood, and marriage are 'based on five facts', which, they expand, are:

> 1) We regularly search our motives and seek to empty ourselves of all that would tarnish true perception of reality. 2) We pray that God would give us humility, teachability, wisdom, insight, fairness, and honesty. 3) We make every effort to submit our minds to the unbending and unchanging grammatical and historical reality of the Biblical texts in Greek and Hebrew, using the best methods of study available to get as close as possible to the intentions of the Biblical writers. 4) We test our conclusions by the history of exegesis to reveal any chronological snobbery or cultural myopia. 5) We test our conclusions in the real world of contemporary ministry and look for resonance from mature and godly people.
>
> (Piper and Grudem 2006: 84–85)

Taken all together, this (research of Hebrew and Greek, consultation of 'mature and godly people', and claims to 'true perception', 'wisdom', and 'best methods') asserts a high degree of confidence and (self-)righteousness in terms of representing God's will and the Bible.

In some ways, RBMW is less blunt than Köstenberger's succinct pamphlet. For instance, RBMW goes to some length to acknowledge value and virtue in the single life,[19] and does not explicitly depict childlessness and infertility as consequences of sin.[20] Indeed, RBMW, quotes Elisabeth Elliot whose words Piper and Grudem say they prefer to quote 'rather than try (in vain) to improve':

> The gift of virginity, given to every one to offer back to God for His use, is a priceless and irreplaceable gift. It can be offered in the pure sacrifice of marriage, or it can be offered in the sacrifice of a life's celibacy. Does this sound just too, too high and holy? But think for a moment – because the virgin has never known a man, she is free to concern herself wholly with the Lord's affairs, as Paul said in 1 Corinthians 7, 'and her aim in life is to make herself holy, in body and spirit.' She keeps her heart as the Bride of Christ in a very special sense, and offers to the Heavenly Bridegroom alone all that she is and has. When she gives herself willingly to Him in love she has no need to justify herself to the world or to Christians who plague her with questions and suggestions. In a way not open to the married woman her daily 'living sacrifice' is a powerful and humble witness, radiating love. I believe she may enter into the 'mystery' more deeply than the rest of us.
>
> (Elliot, cited in RBMW 2006: 89)

Elliot's words reflect a preoccupation with, even fetishisation of, *female* virginity. Piper may assert and extol the virginity of Jesus (Piper 2006: xix)[21] but it is clearly *female* virginity that is emphasised here, as it tends to be elsewhere – and by no means only in purity culture and evangelical contexts (cf. Stiebert 2022b).

Both RBMW and Köstenberger argue insistently that divinely intended gender roles are natural and clear but that the world now, through defiance against these roles, is a chaotic and dangerous place. Gender roles, they allege, are clearly defined, and assigned in the Bible as the foundation for social life.[22] Now they have become confused and this, in turn, they assert, can lead only to iniquity. Hence, in RBMW we read, 'Confusion over the meaning of sexual personhood today is epidemic. The consequence of this confusion is ... more divorce, more homosexuality, more sexual abuse, more promiscuity, more social awkwardness, and more emotional distress and suicide that come with the loss of God-given identity' (Piper 2006: 33).[23] In contrast, these sources assert, the Bible is unambiguous: hence, RBMW speaks of 'the clarity of Scripture' and the 'plain meanings of Biblical texts', which have become

16 Biblical Marriage

obscured by 'hermeneutical oddities' and 'technical ingenuity', which pose a 'threat to Biblical authority' and 'accessibility of ... meaning' (Piper and Grudem, RBMW 2006: 89). Köstenberger adds that the institutions of marriage and family are 'under siege today' and that 'only a return to the biblical foundation' can 'reverse the[ir] decline ... in our culture' (Köstenberger 2011: 2). Biblical marriage, as expounded by RBMW and FRC, is the solution to this troubling chaos: if the Bible is read, interpreted, and followed properly (i.e., in the ways *they* promote – not in alternative ways, which may be ingenious but are ultimately wrong and, therefore, unnatural, and ungodly), then, and only then, things will have their proper place in society.[24]

Both argue that the foundation is two complementary sexes, male and female, with each having clearly defined roles. Köstenberger adds that '[t]he very fact' that in some homosexual couples one partner takes on a 'male' and the other a 'female' role – as 'attested by two different Greek words for homosexuality in the New Testament' – 'provides indirect support for the complementarity inherent in the divine creation design' (Köstenberger 2011: 16).[25] Apparently, complementarianism is the will of God, and it is also 'natural'. Both subscribe to a 'different but equal' complementarianism: 'One can possess a different function and still be equal in essence and worth' (Schreiner, RBMW 2006: 128).[26] This prescribes that men have responsibility for leadership – in marriage, in the family, and in wider society, including in church settings. Concerning the latter, RBMW states 'the Bible teaches that only men should be pastors and elders (Piper and Grudem, RBMW 2006: 60) and, moreover, that 'it is unbiblical ... and therefore detrimental, for women to assume this role' (Piper and Grudem, RBMW 2006: 61). The question as to why a woman who feels called to be pastor shouldn't become one, is answered with, 'We do not believe God genuinely calls women to be pastors. We say this not because we can read the private experience of anyone, but because we believe private experience must always be assessed by the public criterion of God's Word, the Bible' (Piper and Grudem, RBMW 2006: 77). And, by implication, they *can* interpret this divine Word accurately and overrule any protestations of inequality. Women are assigned other, different tasks, including being 'helpers'[27] to men and nurturing children.[28] Concessions are few and, ultimately, only underscore these roles. As Piper states:

> A woman is not unduly masculine in performing these things [i.e. giving moral and spiritual *leadership*, taking initiative in *providing* the bread of life, and *protecting* from the greatest enemies of all, Satan and sin] for her children if she has the sense that this would be properly done by her husband if she had one, and if she performs them with a uniquely feminine demeanor.

> However, if a woman undertakes to give this kind of leadership toward her husband she would not be acting in a properly feminine way, but would

be taking up the masculine calling in that relationship. If the husband is there but neglects his responsibility and does not provide leadership for the children, then the mature, feminine mother will make every effort to do so, yet in a way that says to the husband, 'I do not defy you, I love you and long with all my heart that you were with me in this spiritual and moral commitment, leading me and the family to God'.

(Piper, RBMW 2006: 37)

For Piper, a woman must maintain her submissive 'feminine demeanor' and a man has a 'masculine calling' to lead; such an allocation of roles is 'a natural and good penchant given by God' (Piper, RBMW 2006: 52). Even when a husband is irresponsible and neglectful, a wife is to submit to him and to refrain from taking the lead (Piper, RBMW 2006: 47). Instead of confrontation, or assuming leadership, Piper advises feminine persuasion for women, and raises up Abigail (1 Samuel 25) for her 'amazing restraint and submissiveness and discretion' (Piper, RBMW 2006: 52). Abigail was the wife of Nabal (Hebrew for 'fool') who went behind her husband's back to placate David, later going on to become David's wife, after Nabal (conveniently) drops dead.[29]

Going into great detail in his chapter (with the subtitle 'Manhood and Womanhood Defined According to the Bible'), Piper explains how 'a man' and how 'a woman' should act and be (Piper, RBMW 2006: 54–58). Women should 'not fritter away [their] time on soaps or women's magazines or unimportant hobbies or shopping', while men are to avoid 'excessive sports and recreation or unimportant hobbies or aimless diddling in the garage' (Piper, RBMW 2006: 55). He goes on to cite J. I. Packer's 'perceptive observation': 'a situation in which a female boss has a male secretary, or a marriage in which the woman (as we say) wears the trousers, will put more strain on the humanity of both parties than if it were the other way around. This is part of the reality of the creation, a given fact that nothing will change' (cited in Piper, RBMW 2006: 45).

RBMW is just as firm about representing 'the reality of creation' and 'God's will' (Piper, RBMW 2006: 47–48). Again, what is deemed 'natural' is also what God wants and, by extension, what the Bible prescribes. Hence, so Piper, 'when we follow [God's] idea of marriage (sketched in texts like Genesis 2:18–24; Proverbs 5:15–19; 31:10–31;[30] Mark 10:2–12; Ephesians 5:21–33; Colossians 3:18–19; and 1 Peter 3:1–7) we are most satisfied and he is most glorified' (Piper, RBMW 2006: 53). Female submission is called in RBMW the '*disposition to yield*', implying it is an inherent trait. But it is also described as 'a wife's *divine calling* to honor and affirm her husband's leadership' (Piper and Grudem 2006: 61, italics added), once more linking 'nature' with divine will.

In terms of using the Bible, a proof-texting approach of selecting and applying, as well as twisting and supplementing, verses and passages to

18 *Biblical Marriage*

promote ideologies of gender determinism, anti-feminism, anti-homosexuality, and anti-gender fluidity is very apparent. In this vein, Köstenberger distils out and hones in on six iniquities. These iniquities, he claims, have emerged from 'humanity's rebellion against the Creator's purposes' and comprise polygamy, divorce, adultery, homosexuality, sterility, and gender role confusion (Köstenberger 2011: 8). But Köstenberger's representation of the Bible's content is dodgy. Strikingly, in the Hebrew Bible itself, polygamy and divorce do not seem to pose much of a problem.[31] Köstenberger justifies monogamy on account of the creation story, where 'God only made Eve', even though 'it was certainly within [his] prerogative and power to make more than one wife for the man' (Köstenberger 2011: 9). But all the many polygamous marriages after this, he decides, even those of men depicted as favoured, chosen, and blessed by God (such as Abraham, Jacob, or David) fall short of the divine ideal.[32] Köstenberger also notes that divorce became 'so common that it had to be regulated in the Mosaic code' (Köstenberger 2011: 9), which he finds regrettable rather than an indication of divorce being depicted as accepted and legally accommodated. Köstenberger overlooks, or ignores, that polygamy and divorce (just like enslavement and rape of enslaved persons) are commonplace and unproblematic in parts of the Bible.

Continuing with his list of iniquities, adultery indeed appears as a dreadful crime in the Bible: a man who has sex with any woman betrothed or married to someone other than himself, and a woman who has sex with anyone other than her husband or husband-to-be (the gendered double-standard is clear), are strongly condemned in some biblical texts (e.g., Lev 20:10; Deut 22:22). If a man rapes a virginal woman who is *not* betrothed or married to another man, he pays a fine and marries her, without possibility of divorce (Deut 22:28–29). Enslaved persons appear to be sexually available to the men who 'own' them.[33] If they are 'designated' or 'acquired' for a man, any sexual interference by another man can be fixed with a ceremonial offering (Lev 19:20–22). This does *not* suggest monogamy for anyone other than married women and suggests acceptance of male sexual predation and no concept of consent. However, such examples of male power and abuse are *not* identified by Köstenberger as iniquities or as indications of fallen nature.

Next in the list is sterility, which is always understood in the Bible as a female deficiency. Sterility is depicted as lamentable and often as something that is alleviated by God (who 'opens the womb') to herald a special child. Sarah's, Rebekah's, Rachel's, Hannah's, and Manoah's wife's infertility, for instance, are all brought to an end with the birth of a son who carries a special blessing. Punishment for personal sin or consequence of fallen nature are not, however, emphasised in any of these stories.

Köstenberger's case for a biblical basis for the 'iniquities' of homosexuality and gender role confusion is especially weak. Quite simply, the Bible has little, if anything, to say on either. Arguably, what we call 'homosexuality' nowadays, namely a sexual orientation, is not represented at all in the Bible – as opposed to same-sex sex-acts, which receive isolated pejorative mention (most clearly with regard to male-male rape at Gen 19:5 and Judg 19:22; and at Lev 18:22; 20:13; Rom 1:26–27).[34] There is certainly not anything like the preoccupation with same-sex sexuality and sex-acts that is in evidence today (cf. Gevisser 2020). Likewise, the Bible reflects some indications of gender roles (as well as suggestions of fluidity, exceptions, and shifts over time), and there is a legal text describing someone who cross-dresses as abominable to God (Deut 22:5) – but, again, there is all up very little said on the matter in the Bible.[35] Köstenberger, like the authors of RBMW, is fixated on the evils of all of feminism, homosexuality, and what he calls gender role confusion. Again, it appears that Köstenberger decides what it is he rejects before plumbing the Bible for proof-texts to support his agenda. His agenda is then packaged in many assertions about the importance and authority of the Bible, about nature, and God's will, as well as in careful and selective use of biblical verses.[36]

Sometimes, RBMW and Köstenberger quote the Bible and what it says is emphasised (in some cases, arguably, *over*emphasised). Hence, there is a very frequent and insistent reference made to the story of Adam and Eve in Genesis 2–3. In RBMW it even states, 'as Genesis 1–3 go, so goes the whole Biblical debate. One way or the other, all the additional Biblical texts on manhood and womanhood must be interpreted consistently with these chapters. They lay the very foundation of Biblical manhood and womanhood' (Ortlund, RBMW 2006: 95). Here, one woman (Eve) is created to be the companion of one man (Adam),[37] and prior to this humanity is told to be fruitful and multiply (Gen 1:28). Extraordinarily, this story is used to justify all of monogamy; heteronormativity; heterosexual, monogamous, sexually exclusive marriage to the exclusion of all other kinds of marriage; female submission to male headship; and procreation. It is also used to condemn homosexuality, non-binary gender,[38] transgender, polygamy, feminism, abortion, divorce, and, though less often, single life, elective childlessness, and women's ordination. Wow. For a short mythological story, featuring an anthropomorphic deity, a talking serpent, and magical fruit, in a biblical book that makes no claims to divine authorship or inspiration, a story which never makes any explicit reference to marriage, let alone feminism,[39] or homosexuality, this is quite something… Something much more straightforwardly defended on the basis of a literalist reading of the text – namely, incest – receives no mention at all in RBMW, because – of course – incest does not fit the ideological agenda.[40]

Let us expand briefly on just one example of how the story of Adam and Eve is manipulated in RBMW to serve the ideology of complementarianism and male headship. Piper and Grudem identify the serpent of Genesis with Satan. This is imported into Genesis where the serpent is not named and is described only as 'shrewd' – not as evil, or satanic (Gen 3:1). The identification is not, however, invented by the contributors but goes back to the Greek Bible (Rev 12:9; 20:2). They write,

> We think that Satan's main target was not Eve's peculiar gullibility (if she had one), but rather Adam's headship as the one ordained by God to be responsible for the life of the garden. Satan's subtlety is that he knew the created order God had ordained for the good of the family, and he deliberately defied it by ignoring the man and taking up his dealings with the woman. Satan put her in the position of spokesman, leader, and defender. At that moment both the man and the woman slipped from their innocence and let themselves be drawn into a pattern of relating that to this day has proved destructive.
>
> (Piper and Grudem, RBMW 2006: 73)[41]

So: the serpent is Satan and knew of 'Adam's headship' and of 'the created order God had ordained for the good of the family' – even before these were (according to the story itself) divinely ordained (Gen 3:16) and before there was a family (Gen 4:1–2). Moreover, female leadership in defiance of rightful male headship is what is blamed, alongside Satan's subtlety, for setting in motion something that has 'proved destructive' up to this day. The interpretation is the vehicle for complementarian ideology, and it uses, or better, manipulates and adds into, the story in highly selective ways. Hence, social values and directives do not so much arise from the text as the text is applied to *construct* them; or, the text is not here guiding people, but rather, people (in this case the authors of RBMW) are guiding the text.

While sometimes in complementarian interpretation the biblical text is claimed to be clear-cut and unmovable, on other occasions, there is some allowance for cultural malleability, but again in the service of promoting the conservative complementarian agenda. Hence, as we saw, much is made (rather assuredly) of how the early chapters of Genesis dictate male headship, female submission, and clear-cut gender roles that envisage a particular 'brand' of femininity and masculinity. But then Thomas Schreiner argues that Paul's injunction (in 1 Cor 11:2–16), for women to wear head coverings while praying and prophesying, is *not* literal in intention but is *really* about dress and conduct *culturally appropriate* for feminine women. Consequently, Paul is *not* requiring women nowadays to wear head coverings, or disallowing present-day women to wear jeans or trousers (Schreiner, RBMW 2006: 138). Instead, Schreiner argues, Paul is *really* on about women expressing 'a demeanor that is humble and submissive to male leadership' (Schreiner 2006: 132). This is because – then as now – women 'appropriating leadership' goes hand in hand with 'loss of femininity' (Schreiner 2006: 139) – and that (unlike wearing head coverings) *is* binding, because the Bible says so (!).

Piper and Grudem, too, distinguish between texts with 'limited application' and texts that articulate 'an abiding requirement': the former is culturally

Biblical Marriage 21

specific, while the latter is 'rooted in the nature of God, the gospel, or the created order' (RBMW 2006: 74). And it is *they* who, like Schreiner, can make the call as to which is which. So ... the Bible *does* say that women should wear head coverings while praying (1 Cor 11:5, 13) and should not wear men's garments (Deut 22:5) – but it is not *actually* necessary for women *nowadays* to wear head coverings while praying, or to eschew jeans. But Schreiner stresses husbands' headship over their wives (1 Cor 11:3) and prescribes for women an attitude and demeanour that is humble and submissive – because this is God's *permanent* will and his created order.

The authors in RBMW are certainly not ignorant of the biblical text: indeed, they cite it widely, often with analysis of Hebrew or Greek terminology. They do, however, employ the text to fit their ideology. In doing so, they sometimes argue that the text is clear and unequivocal (including about matters not by any means explicit or even notionally present in the biblical text itself – such as elective abortion,[42] or transgender); other times, they argue the biblical text is culturally shaped and needs to be interpreted differently in the present (which is why veiling is not required for women and why women *can* wear trousers); other times again, the text is read very flexibly, with certain bits suppressed entirely, to square apparent contradictions with RBMW authors' ideology.

Regarding frictions between, on the one hand, what biblical texts state and, on the other, complementarian ideology, Grudem and Piper attempt to tackle the rather glaring biblical references to female leadership. Miriam, for instance, is, as they note, called a prophet. They argue, however, that she 'focused her ministry, as far as we can tell, on the women of Israel (Exodus 15:20)'[43] (Piper and Grudem, RBMW 2006: 72), and this, somehow, makes her leadership acceptable, because she is not leading men. Women leading men, apparently, would violate the divine scheme.[44] Deborah, meanwhile, is in the Bible called not only a prophet, but also a woman/wife, a judge, and a mother in Israel (Judg 4:4; 5:7). Her leadership as prophet and judge over Israel is, again, not accepted by the authors of RBMW – not even as an exception among judges – and they do not praise Deborah. Instead, they refer to her as, 'a living indictment of the weakness of Barak and other men in Israel who should have been more courageous leaders (Judges 4:9)' (Piper and Grudem, RBMW 2006: 72). The female prophet Huldah, meanwhile, they acknowledge, 'evidently exercised her prophetic gift' but 'not in a public preaching ministry but by means of private consultation (2 Kings 22:14–20)' (Piper and Grudem, RBMW 2006: 72). Again, this, by implication, makes female prophecy acceptable – because it is private and not (publicly?) carried out where it might undermine male leadership. Deborah's leadership, on the other hand, was very much public: she received 'the Israelites' to make judgements (Judg 4:5) and went into battle (Judg 4:9–10). She is praised in song (Judg 5) and her rule leads to forty years of quiet (Judg 5:31). Despite her ostensibly positive depiction in the biblical text, the authors of RBMW nevertheless deem

22 *Biblical Marriage*

Deborah's reign not to have been an example of good leadership by a woman but an indictment on men (above all Barak); consequently, *despite what the text says*, they consider it to be, ultimately, negatively critical of female leadership. Miriam and Huldah, meanwhile, are positively acknowledged by them as prophets, but this time focusing closely on what the text *does* say: this is because these women keep their prophecy confined to women's spheres (Miriam), or private and domestic spheres (Huldah). Piper and Grudem add, moreover, 'We must also keep in mind that God's granting power or revelation to a person is no sure sign that this person is an ideal model for us to follow in every respect. This is evident, for example, from the fact that some of those God blessed in the Old Testament were polygamists (e.g., Abraham and David). Not even the gift of prophecy is proof of a person's obedience and endorsement by God' (Piper and Grudem, RBMW 2006: 72). This last comment seems to acknowledge that the Bible is tricky to interpret. It also shows that what *they* decide is proper (e.g., monogamy and male leadership) can overrule what the text plainly says (i.e., that polygyny was freely practised without obvious reproof, and that Deborah led Israel successfully). In other words, for all the emphasis placed on the importance and authority of the Bible, and the assertions as to its plain meaning, the authors of RBMW treat the biblical text selectively, strategically, and sometimes very flexibly, whichever way fits their agenda.

The Bible, quite simply, does not 'speak' or 'say' anything. It is *not* the case that if we just 'listen right' its meaning held *in* the text clearly emerges. Instead, we read and interpret *out* anything we call meaning. And this is determined by the selections we make, as well as by what we are seeking. Complementarianism has a method: biblical texts are brought into line with a predetermined ideology according to which wives are to be above all submissive to their husbands, never competing with or challenging them, and, in addition, homemakers, child raisers, and attractive. A prime example is Proverbs 31:10–31, the 'most complete portrait we have of a marriage' (Hunter 2011: 8). The text (in the NRSV) begins with the question, 'A capable wife who can find?' This acrostic poem is sometimes characterised along the lines of being about a 'good wife'. The woman is clearly admired and praised – her worth exceeds that of precious stones (traditionally rubies, 31:10). But this wife seems only partially like the wife of complementarian ideals. Yes, she takes good care of her husband (31:11–12), supports his success and status (31:23), and performs some tasks typically associated with domestic chores, such as handcrafts with textiles (31:13, 19, 22, 24). But she is also presented as a powerful and independent *'eshet-chayil*, a woman, or wife, of strength, valour, or power (31:10).[45] The translation of 'capable wife' conceals the fact that the descriptive noun *chayil* regularly refers to male physical strength, the kind of brawn and power typifying warriors (e.g., Jos 1:14; Judg 6:12; 2 Kgs 5:1).[46] A second word of strength, *'oz*, is also applied to her (31:17, 25), and again, this descriptor does not fit well with the feminine ideal of

Biblical Marriage 23

complementarianism. Moreover, far from just staying home and weaving, she is also a trader (31:24), who travels afar (31:14), and some kind of realtor who also performs physical labour (31:16).[47] One of the fullest accounts in the Bible of what a desirable wife is like hardly aligns with the 'feminine demeanor' described elsewhere in RBMW.

Deborah, we saw, whose role as leader and warrior cannot easily be played down, is critiqued in RBMW, because she does not fit into the complementarian scheme. The woman of Proverbs 31, on the other hand, is clearly a wife and praised for this at some length. Consequently, there may be more at stake in terms of fitting her into the complementarian frame. In order to do so, the woman's physical power, with its associations of military prowess, as well as her dominance in the household (called hers, not her husband's, 31:15) and beyond, is downplayed. Instead, RBMW calls her prudent and 'a godly heroine' (Patterson, RBMW 2006: 367), as well as (with rather capitalist overtones now!) 'a visionary investor' (Patterson, RBMW 2006: 368). The question is raised in RBMW if a wife and mother working outside the home can be acceptable if 'beneficial to her family, ... aid[ing] her husband in his calling' (Knight, RBMW 2006: 348). In answer, there is reference to 'her primary calling to be wife and mother' and the claim is made (without the biblical text itself actually offering any insight into the woman's perspective – if she even *is* a real woman)[48] that she 'has not sought to "find herself" or to make her own career' (Knight, RBMW 2006: 348).[49] RBMW concludes that 'some types of leadership and management by women harmonize with a husband's more ultimate leadership' (Poythress, RBMW 2006: 245) and that there is in Proverbs 31 'no mention of rights or pursuit of self-serving interests; neither is the husband assigned to domestic pursuits' (Patterson, RBMW 2006: 367) and also that 'there is no hint in the passage that she had any other purpose than to meet the needs of her family in the best possible way' (Patterson, 2006: 369). In other words, the poem is brought (bent?) into line with complementarianism. The possibly awkward elements of the woman's independence and work outside the household must therefore be attributed to her tireless devotion and work for her husband's good. Not only this, RBMW manages to bring in also that this woman has feminine physical charms. The text itself may say that 'beauty is vain' (31:30), but RBMW finds a way to argue that 'God's woman does give time and effort to her appearance' (Patterson, RBMW 2006: 369), because 'she undoubtedly used the fine flax or linen cloth that was the best of the day, and purple garments, indicating wealth or high rank, which were rare indeed' (Patterson, RBMW 2006: 369). In passing and for good measure, RBMW approvingly cites a passage that says of an admired preacher's admired wife that 'she stayed attractive, and fifteen years later she was still able to entrance men much younger than she was' (Patterson, RBMW 2006: 369). What emerges from this is that a probably capitalist-infused religious ideology that admires wealth (visionary investment, fabrics indicating high rank), alongside women's submission and attractiveness determines the interpretation of Proverbs 31:10–31, resulting in the emphasis of certain elements over the suppression of others, alongside the weaving in of complementarian strands.

We authors acknowledge that we hold ideologies, too, and that these are feminist. We do not always recognise the feminism reviled in RBMW, which is characterised as aggressive, and as motivating women to wrest headship from men, thereby depriving boys and girls of what God wants them to be, and inciting depravity and abuse. Ortlund asks, with 'feminist ideals ... aggressively pursued throughout our society – how is it that, under these conditions, sexual exploitation and confusion and perversity have exploded in incidence?' (Ortlund, RBMW 2006: 105). Again, feminism and non-normative gender, alongside a distortion of male headship (namely, 'male domination') are blamed: they are aggressive, exploitative, confused, perverse, and rampant. Male headship and female submission, on the other hand, are the answer, and deemed natural, God-ordained, and biblical.[50] Ortlund does not describe or cite evidence for the incidence explosion of vile things that seem to have emanated from pervasive feminism. He also does not explain why (certainly in the USA and UK) domestic violence (like divorce) is as prevalent in Bible-using Jewish and Christian populations as in the general public, nor why sexual abuse has been shown to be rampant in religious institutions, including conservative Christian ones (see Brown 2009; Everhart 2020). Furthermore, there is nothing all too new about sexual abuse in Christian-run institutions, which predates the wave of second wave feminism (see Lynch 2021) and has long and deep roots reaching very far back.[51] RBMW also charges evangelical feminists (the target of this book, as is clear from its subtitle) with 'reinterpret[ing] the sacred canon that exists to suit their purposes' (Ortlund, RBMW 2006: 111).[52] But this is also exactly what RBMW and Köstenberger are doing – for all their protestations of channelling God and depicting 'the truth' or true biblical manhood and womanhood.

Our ideals are feminist in that we believe in equal opportunity for self-fulfilment, regardless of sex, sexual identity, or orientation, as well as in equal pay for equal work.[53] Equality, let alone equity, which we consider aspirations, are not, apparently, motivations for all portions of the Bible. Hence, great swaths of the Bible take social hierarchies, including being born into privilege (e.g., to a royal house or to a priestly clan) and subservience of enslaved persons, for granted. Moreover, there are clear inequalities between ethnic groups of people, with Moabites and Ammonites in the Hebrew Bible (e.g., Deut 23:3) and Samaritans in the Greek Bible understood to be inherently inferior or deficient in some way (which is why Jesus' story of the Good Samaritan in Luke 10:30–37 is so subversive). Equality also gets rather poor press in RBMW. Here Ortlund writes,

> Consider the obvious: God ... does not value equality in finances, talents, and opportunity. It is God who deliberately ordains inequalities in many

aspects of our lives. When I came from the womb, I had only so much potential for physical, intellectual, and aesthetic development. Some are born with less than I was, others with more. Because God is ultimately the One who shapes our lives, I have to conclude that God is not interested in unlimited equality among us. And because God is also wise, I further conclude that unlimited equality must be a false ideal. But the Bible does teach the equal personhood and value and dignity of all the human race – men, women, and children – and that must be the only equality that matters to God.

(Ortlund, RBMW 2006: 100)

He continues that 'equal rights' may sound noble, then asks,

does God really grant husbands and wives equal rights *in an unqualified sense*? Surely God confers upon them equal worth as His image-bearers. But does a wife possess under God all the rights that her husband has *in an unqualified sense*? As the head, the husband bears the primary responsibility to lead their partnership in a God-glorifying direction. Under God, a wife may not compete for that primary responsibility. It is her husband's just because he is the husband, by the wise decree of God. The ideal of 'equal rights' in an unqualified sense is not Biblical.

(Ortlund, RBMW 2006: 105)

Ortlund is speaking very confidently ('surely') and purports to know what matters to God and what constitutes his 'wise decree'. He accepts that inequalities – in terms of wealth and ability and looks – just *are* and are therefore reflections of how (unequal!) God wants things to be.[54] Ortlund, maintains that equality and equal rights are not biblical or godly whereas equal worth is. How the two – unequal rights and opportunities alongside equal worth – coexist in practice is not entirely clear, nor is the potential for harm posed by this lack of clarity acknowledged. *Who* decides what the 'responsibility' of headship allows or restricts? *Who* decides what is 'a God-glorifying direction'? Ortlund takes another shot at feminism stating, 'Feminists seem to be reasoning that, because *some* subordination is degrading, *all* subordination must necessarily be degrading. On the contrary, what Biblical headship requires and what slave-holding forbids is that the head respect the helper as an equally significant person in the image of God' (Ortlund, RBMW 2006: 104). But what is it to be 'equally significant', or to have equal worth, if one is subordinated, with deprivation of rights? What is the value of 'worth' if it constricts agency, desire, and fulfilment? If, for example, subordination makes it impossible for a wife to control her own fertility, or to follow a vocation or career she desires, or to express her full range of feelings, then 'equal worth' becomes worthless. The scope for coerciveness and for abuse of a man's 'responsibility' and God-ordained 'headship' is not just rather obvious, it is also well attested.[55]

> I have been working with a woman who tells me she was taught and believes that in the home the husband is God. Obedience to one's husband is, she believes, a way of worship, of serving her husband and her God, and a way to earn a place in heaven. Disobedience can bring the punishment of hell not only for herself but for men in her family – particularly her husband. So, she feels guilty and that keeps her compliant. She even feels guilty just talking to me. She admits to suffering and to being afraid and miserable in her marriage – but these things run very deep. Her faith and her efforts to live in compliance with her faith are very powerful. The presence of laws doesn't really help in many cases. Often laws are characterised as 'secular', with religious law overriding secular law. Adherence to religious law over secular law is even seen as a proof of faithfulness to God. One woman I am working with acknowledged her husband's abuse and abandonment. But he had made her swear on her sacred book that she would not report him to the police. She will not budge from this oath, and I know that if I suggested it I would lose her trust.
>
> (Saima)

Feminism and a decline in biblical literacy are blamed in RBMW for departures from biblical marriage, for high divorce rates, and for diverse forms of abuse and intimate partner violence, but the reality, as already mentioned, that divorce, domestic and sexual abuse and violence are, certainly in Western contexts, as high in Bible-reading and -using Christian communities as in the wider population, is not fully acknowledged. Instead, in RBMW, Köstenberger, and LLF, 'biblical marriage' is idealised. To give just one clear example, marriage is described as '[a]t its very heart ... not a human custom ... [but] a divinely created institution, defined for all ages and all cultures ... the profound fusion of two lives into one, shared life together, by the mutual consent and covenant of marriage ... the complete and permanent giving over of oneself into a new circle of shared existence with one's partner' (Ortlund, RBMW 2006: 101). All envisage this institution in heteronormative terms; and none engages adequately, let alone fully, with the reality of abuse in marriage, or with the very many biblical passages that associate violence and marriage.[56]

Köstenberger refers to various 'sins' that have corrupted marriage – among these are polygamy, divorce, and adultery, but not domestic violence. There is one mention of intimate partner violence where Köstenberger states, 'marital separation (though not necessarily divorce) may be needed in cases of persistent spousal abuse' (Köstenberger 2011: 19). This indicates, first, that divorce is so grievous that it is preferable to put up with (some) spousal abuse to avoid it; second, that divorce, rather than anything that might lead up to it (such as coercive control, or domestic abuse and violence) constitutes the sin to be avoided;[57] and third, that spousal abuse needs to be 'persistent' before it really counts and before separation is ever advisable. RBMW also does not deny abuse (Piper, RBMW 2006: 42), deplores its occurrence (Elliot, RBMW 2006: 397), and expresses concern at rising rates (Appendix to RBMW 2006: 469). Yet domestic violence and abuse do not appear among the many references to 'biblical marriage' to give space to the numerous biblical depictions associating violence and marriage. These depictions include the text where a soldier desires to marry a beautiful captive woman (Deut 21:10–14), the battered wife metaphors (Ezek 16:37–42; 23:47; Hos 2:3–7), and accounts of rape 'marriage' (Num 31:18; Judg 21:12, 19–23). The idea that abuse could arise as a symptom of prescribing male headship and female submission, or of staying in an unhappy marriage, is not entertained in RBMW. Instead, 'proper' male headship and 'proper' female submission are described as Christ-like (Piper and Grudem, RBMW 2006: 62); abuse is described as the result of improper maintenance of godly order, and feminism is blamed for occurrences of abuse (e.g. Piper and Grudem, RBMW 2006: 62). There are also references to the 'myth of male predominance in domestic abuse' and claims that attempts to air such 'myths' encounter threats from feminists (Ayers, RBMW 2006: 314). And yet, the genderedness of domestic abuse and preponderance of male perpetrators are widely attested.[58]

This chapter has shown that 'biblical marriage' relies on selective passages, or proof-texting, from the Bible, and on assertions that these passages constitute God's true word, fixed and valid for all time. In the passage quoted above, Piper and Grudem, consequently, speak of the 'unbending and unchanging ... reality of the Biblical texts', and Köstenberger states firmly: 'Marriage and the family were God's idea, and as divine institutions they are not open to human renegotiation or revision. As we have seen, the Bible clearly teaches that God instituted marriage as a covenant between one man and one woman, a lifelong union of two partners...' (Köstenberger 2011: 20). There is no room for negotiation here. 'Biblical marriage' claims to distil what the Bible *actually says and means* concerning marriage. It is, however, a predetermined ideology, packaged up with other ideologies that promote purity culture and reject feminism, abortion, and LGBTQ+ orientation, identity, and rights. Verses from the Bible are selected to shore up this ideology, and much of the rest of its 'argument' is made through strong assertions. So, the upshot is rather like saying, '(selections from) the Bible say what I believe and therefore confirm what I believe', or '(selections from) the Bible say what I argue is correct and therefore the Bible is correct'.[59]

We will look next at other passages in the Bible that have something to say about marriage, to get a fuller picture of what is often suppressed by biblical marriage – for all its claims to biblical verity. To be clear, however, we are not doing this with a view to creating our own biblical blueprint; we do not seek to promote biblical authority uncritically – since the Bible has plenty to say – often with apparent, even brutal, clarity – that we firmly reject. We do not advocate sacrificing daughters in order to fulfil an oath to God (Judges 11), or stoning sons who have acted disobediently (Deut 21:18–21); we reject the subjection of women to ordeals that probe their marital fidelity (Num 5), or their virginity at the time of marriage, as well as the death penalty for perceived sexual misconduct (Deut 22:13–21); just as we abhor the notion of women having to marry their rapists (Deut 21:11–13; 22:28–29), or the sanctification of rape following warfare (Num 31:18ff.). The associations between marriage and violence will be the focus of the next chapter.

Notes

1. See, https://cbmw.org/about/mission-vision/ (accessed 12 February 2021). We make occasional reference, too, to an earlier publication with the cooperation of CBMW, edited by Grudem (2002).
2. See, https://www.frc.org/brochure/the-bibles-teaching-on-marriage-and-family (accessed 12 February 2021). The FRC is definite and uncompromising on what this worldview means qua marriage (see https://www.frc.org/marriage, accessed 18 February 2021).
3. For a superb and nuanced discussion informed by qualitative research, see Shorter (2021). Shorter is careful to consider the divergent ways complementarian religion and discourse are regarded from within, by professing complementarians, and from without, by researchers.
4. LLF, like CBMW and FRC, is more than a book, offering online resources and a learning hub. See, https://www.churchofengland.org/resources/living-love-and-faith/living-love-and-faith-learning-hub (accessed 18 February 2021).
5. Numerous other churches and religious organisations could also be drawn in here, notably the Roman Catholic Church. The International Academy for Marital Spirituality (INTAMS) is rooted in Catholicism. Its journal *Marriage, Families & Spirituality* provides many examples of exploring marriage from various theological and biblical perspectives. Gevisser notes, 'the two regions where Catholicism was dominant – Europe and Latin America' have become battlegrounds on same-sex marriage: e.g., Argentina (2010), and Ireland (2015) (Gevisser 2020: 217).
6. It was a Conservative–Liberal Democrat coalition Parliament that in 2013 passed the Marriage (Same Sex Couples) Act introducing civil marriage for same-sex couples in England and Wales. At the time of writing, the CofE upholds that 'the Christian understanding and doctrine of marriage as a lifelong union between one man and one woman remains unchanged' (Welby and Sentamu 2017). In February 2023, amid much controversy from polarised sides, the CofE permitted the blessing of same-sex unions, stopping short of naming them marriages. A 2022 YouGov poll (following polls conducted in 2013, 2016, and 2020) commissioned by the Ozanne Foundation to ascertain attitudes to same-sex marriage shows an increase among persons self-identifying as Anglican who considers same-sex marriage 'right'. There is now a clear majority of 55% (up from 38% in 2013 and 48% in 2020) (Ozanne 2022). For one view opposing the blessings, see the statement by the Archbishop of the Church of Uganda, which includes the words, 'if it looks like a wedding, and sounds like a wedding… it IS a wedding' (Kaziimba 2023).
7. Grudem is a prominent figure in CBMW and endorsed Donald Trump's policies in both presidential election campaigns. In 2016, he referred to the prospect of Hilary Clinton's victory as 'the imminent triumph of anti-Christian liberal tyranny'

on account of 'her support for abortion rights, government imposition of gender confusion on our children, hate speech laws used to silence Christians, and government-sanctioned exclusion of thousands of Christians from their lifelong occupations because they won't bow to the homosexual agenda' (Grudem 2016: 4). Contributors to both volumes (co-)edited by Grudem (2002, 2006) include persons who in their brief biographies draw attention to serving Republican presidents.

8 On CBMW.ORG the resources under 'Abortion' make clear links between abortion (called a 'sin against God and nature') and the Democratic Party, damning Presidents Biden and Obama, as well as other Democratic representatives, notably Rachel Levine who is a transgender woman but pointedly referred to with male pronouns. The sole female contributor writing on the topic of abortion, who states she has terminated a pregnancy, refers to abortion as not only evil but 'selfish'. The picture that emerges from the CBMW resources is that abortions are performed because women and men care more about such secular things as their education, money, career, reputation, and having fun, than about life, family, and God. Similar criticisms are also regularly levelled at feminists and are again, very easy to locate in any perusal of CBMW or FRC websites. RBMW has as its subtitle, 'A Response to Evangelical Feminism'. More accurately, RBMW is less a response to than a rebuttal of their construction of evangelical feminism. For another discussion on the alleged dangers of feminism and the delights of 'biblical womanhood' by a conservative Christian woman, see Reissig (2015). On tensions between evangelical and feminist frameworks, with a particular focus on spousal abuse, see Haaken, Fussell and Mankowski (2007).

9 There is a vast and spectral literature on each of these topics and on whether and how the Bible mentions or prescribes on matters pertaining to them. This cannot be pursued in any way fully in this book. For a seminal speech referring to these topics and associating them with Republican Party ideology, see Patrick ('Pat') Buchanan's 'Culture War' Speech, the Address to the Republican National Convention in Houston, Texas (1992). The speech is filled with allusions to the Bible, God, and Christian religion. Marriage also features prominently, and Buchanan makes clear he is 'against the amoral idea that gay and lesbian couples should have the same standing in law as married men and women'.

10 One text that illustrates succinctly and accessibly the spectrum of ideological approaches on the topics of homosexuality, Christianity, and the Bible is Holben (1999). Another divisive topic, which in the US context often splits Protestant Right-wing from Catholic Christians, is the death penalty. Again, the Bible is drawn on in distinctive ideological ways by both sides (see Bailey 2005).

11 For a very full discussion of the various meanings of 'ideology', including with reference to the Bible, see Clines (1995: 9–25).

12 One aim of LLF is to engage and wrestle with just such matters. The attempt is praised, but the result is also critiqued for its hesitancy and ineffectuality by, among others, Thatcher (2021).

13 Where feminist criticism of the Bible is concerned, more than two decades ago already Reinhartz commented on the 'ever-increasing flood of articles, monographs, and anthologies' on the subject, as well as on its 'complexity and diversity' (Reinhartz 2000: 43). As she goes on to develop, polyvocality in feminist criticism is very much in evidence even in just one series: namely, the *A Feminist Companion to the Hebrew Bible* series.

14 There is, indeed, plenty of clinical evidence that refutes this, including reflections on clinical assessments of homosexual behaviour in children spanning fifty years (Harris 2003) and empirical behavioural studies (e.g., Alves et al 2016). Johanna's research with LGBTQ+ Ugandan refugees, the majority of whom reported being raised in conservative Christian homes and in environments inculcating observance

of traditional gender roles (see van Klinken et al 2021), also defies this assessment, as does Saima's work as a practitioner over several decades, including with gay and lesbian persons raised in traditional and conservative Muslim homes and communities.

15 It is correct that intimate partner violence (IPV) can be perpetrated by women and/or against men. Other kinds of abuse also break with more common tendencies – e.g., cases of students stalking and harassing their educators, and of children physically harming their parents. Such forms of abuse are no less dreadful for being more uncommon, and seeking help in such situations may prove particularly difficult. Abuse by women and/or against men can still be distinctly gendered (see Sjoberg 2016 and Greenough 2021). Like Paynter (2020: 22) we maintain that where the Bible is weaponised to exert, facilitate, or legitimate abuse it is predominantly by husbands against wives within heterosexual marriages. This accounts for gendered references and generalisations.

16 Social-work literature on domestic abuse published decades ago, states how one indication that a woman is in imminent danger of violent spousal abuse is when a man quotes Paul's command (Eph 5:21–22) that women be subject to their husbands (Dobash and Dobash 1979: 31–47; cf. Elliott 2009: 1633).

17 Ortlund, for instance, writes 'Male headship may be personally repugnant to feminists, but it does have the virtue of explaining the sacred text'. He makes this claim because, for him, the co-creation of male and female in the image of God (Gen 1:26–28) may signify equality, but the naming of humanity as 'man' (his translation of Hebrew *'adam*, elsewhere translated 'humankind', e.g., NRSV and JPS) 'whispers male headship' (2006: 98). He continues, priggishly, 'I am not arguing that one must always use "man" in social and theological discourse to avoid misrepresenting the truth. I am arguing, however, that, in light of Genesis 1:26–27 and 5:1–2, one may not call this linguistic practice unjust or insensitive without impugning the wisdom and goodness of God' (Ortlund 2006: 98). Ortlund is here stating that English 'man' is the best translation for Hebrew *'adam* even though this could misrepresent 'the truth' (presumably, of inclusivity) *and* that the very word 'whispers' of the ideology of male headship he is promoting. This is then emphasised by calling any challenge to this (and by extension all of feminism) a challenge to God's wisdom and goodness. Wow.

18 In terms of humility, Piper acknowledges that his detailed list outlining what biblical manhood and womanhood are, or should be, is 'incomplete and reflects [his] own culture and limitations'. Yet he also claims (rather grandly) that if it is followed it can 'purify and empower [ministry] in a pattern of Biblical obedience' (Piper 2006: 59).

19 See the Foreword by Piper (2006: xvii–xxviii). Piper argues that maintaining biblical manhood and womanhood applies to all humans, married or single. He is uncompromising in that sex is only acceptable in marriage. Köstenberger repeats this, and (in the context of condemning 'homosexuality', which he equates with same-sex sex-acts) adds that 'intercourse that cannot lead to procreation is … unnatural' (Köstenberger 2011: 10). Sex, therefore, belongs exclusively within heterosexual marriage and should properly transpire in procreation. The potential value of singleness is defended by Piper on the model of Jesus who, he confidently asserts, 'never once had sexual intercourse' (Piper 2006: xix). Singleness and celibacy are praised above all on account of the single-minded gift of service they can bring to ministry.

20 For Köstenberger, single life can hold value (Köstenberger 2011: 14–15) but infertility also 'falls short of the fertility desired by the Creator'. As he defends with reference to the Bible, it results either from 'personal sin', or constitutes 'a simple fact of (fallen) nature' (Köstenberger 2011: 10). The violence such an assertion can cause to those who are involuntarily childless should not be underestimated.

21 Piper states confidently, 'The most fully human person who has ever lived, or ever will live, is Jesus Christ, and He never once had sexual intercourse' (Piper 2006: xix). D'Angelo explains that the marital status of Jesus is disputed (D'Angelo 2014: 499). Piper's assertion appears to be based on the following sequence of ideological construction: first, Jesus is the best of humans who follows biblical injunctions fully; second, biblical injunctions permit only sex within monogamous marriage between a man and woman; third, because it says nowhere that Jesus married, he would, therefore, not have had sexual intercourse. The sequence relies on argument from silence, on absence of mention of sexual activity and marriage. Worth considering is the probability that Jesus was sexually abused as part of his torture leading up to crucifixion. This probability is – unlike Piper's assertion – based on what the biblical text *does* say (Mark 15:15–20; Mt 27:26–31; Jn 19:1 and see Tombs 2023: 16–24). Rejection of, or horror at the notion that the stripping, mocking, and scourging of Jesus signify sexual abuse can have the consequence of stigmatising other victims of sexual abuse. Acknowledging Jesus' suffering sexual abuse, on the other hand, can aid fellow survivors towards recovery (see Tombs 2023: 66–80). We raise this to highlight the disturbing potential of biblical depictions and of complementarian interpreters, in fetishising virginity and casting any sexual activity outside of marriage, inclusive of coerced sex and sexual abuse, in terms of impurity.

22 We say 'allege' because a growing body of interpretation argues for ambivalence in biblical depictions of gendered roles. E.g., see Guest (2011) on Jael, and Carden (2006: 52–59) on Joseph, as well as van Klinken et al on Daniel (2021: 5, 154–55). Of course, it can be said that these interpretations promote ideological agendas distinct from those of RBMW – and this is not in dispute. The point is that such cases can and indeed are made by legitimate scholars making credible arguments based also on the biblical text.

23 On the ways that conservative Christian communities and rhetoric, including targeted use of the Bible, inflict transphobic violence, see Blyth and McRae (2018).

24 On 'plain teaching', as used violently 'as a disciplinary technique, silencing other readings of the bible, and enforcing the complementarian model as the only acceptable way of living as a Christian', see Shorter (2021: 240).

25 This argument relies on a predetermined idea of what constitutes 'masculine male' and 'feminine female' and therefore behaviour deemed 'male' or 'female' in a relationship, as well as on an equation of 'homosexuality' (i.e., a sexual orientation) with same-sex sex-acts. It could also be turned around to say that the very existence of homosexuality and same-sex sex-acts in nature also provides 'indirect support' for 'divine creation design'. For all of these arguments, see Holben (1999).

26 'Different but equal' has also been used to justify other inequalities. Piper and Grudem argue that male headship and female submission are completely different from enslavement, for instance, because they are 'rooted in God's act of creation' and in 'the created order of nature' (Piper and Grudem, RBMW 2006: 65). Similar arguments – of divinely ordained rights and privileges of some peoples over others – were, of course, also used by those who justified enslavement and apartheid. Shorter discusses fully how 'different but equal language' can expose hierarchy and inequality and bring about violence but also how it is used both to limit women's participation *and also* to advocate for women's more active involvement (Shorter 2021: 240).

27 Piper understands women's roles as 'helpers' (based on Gen 2:20, *'ezer kenegdô*, translated 'fitting counterpart' in JPS and 'helper as his partner' in NRSV) to refer to 'nurturing strengths and insights that make men stronger and wiser' (Piper, RBMW 2006: 49). Again, interpretation is fitted to suit the ideology where women complement and fit around and support the headship of men. Trible, on the other hand, deems a translation of 'helper' 'misleading', because it 'suggests an assistant,

a subordinate, indeed an inferior'. She argues that the Hebrew word *'ezer* signifies strength, even superiority, and is indeed used to describe God (cf. Hunter 2011: 4). The addition of *kenegdô*, she continues, tempers superiority 'to specify identity, mutuality, and equality… a companion …who alleviates isolation through identity' (Trible 1978: 90). It could be said that both Piper and Trible tailor translation to their ideology, complementarian or feminist.

28 Patterson speaks of 'a woman's natural nesting instinct and maternity', which is once more aligned with values deemed biblical. Patterson claims that 'a salaried job and titled position' stifle women's 'natural' qualities and, 'almost inevitably' lead to failures in mothering (Patterson, RBMW 2006: 365).

29 As ever, the Bible story has been interpreted variously. Some have (like Piper) praised Abigail, including for being 'beautiful inside and out' and for remaining 'focused on God', despite 'suffering in an abusive marriage' (Glahn 2014). Others have noted the fortuitousness of Nabal's sudden death and contemplated a more sinister scenario, according to which Abigail (or Abigail in collusion with David) either precipitated Nabal's heart-attack or murdered him (for references, see O'Rourke Boyle 2001). On the construction of Abigail as the complementarian ideal, and on the disturbing potential of this, with reference to idealising the possibility that she valiantly endured extreme abuse, see Stiebert (forthcoming, 2024).

30 Piper, as quoted above, makes gender-stereotypical claims (e.g., about how women and men fritter away their time), and suggests how women might best adjust their demeanour, submit to, and support their husbands. But this text, characterising and praising a remarkable wife, is possibly at odds with Piper's depiction, in that it portrays the good wife as physically strong (Prov 31:17), as travelling far from her home (31:14), and making business decisions (31:16, 18). But let it also be said that the gendering in Prov 31:10–31 can be problematic for women, including right up to the present (e.g., see Tan 2018: 63–69).

31 For Christians, the Hebrew Bible is the *Old* Testament, namely anterior literature that precedes and predates the gospel ('good news') and covenant of the *New* Testament. It is, however, very widely cited in the literature of the RBMW and FRC – when it suits, that is.

32 Hunter points out regarding polygamy that 'God is never said to disapprove of the practice' (Hunter 2011: 5).

33 Enslavers can also beat enslaved persons without this being punishable – unless beating is fatal (Exod 21:20–21). The Greek Bible prescribes enslaved persons' absolute obedience and forbearance (Eph 6:5; Col 3:22).

34 On the diverse interpretations of all these passages, see Holben (1999).

35 What *is* there in the Bible, moreover, can be, and has been, read in multiple, including gender-diversity-celebrating ways. Hence, there are approving references in the Bible to eunuchs (Hebrew *saris*, Greek *eunouchos*), such as Isa 56:3–5 and Acts 8:27–39. Eunuchs are, possibly, persons who would today be referred to as intersex, or gender-ambivalent, or non-normative males, or queer, and these passages are sometimes read as affirming in queer communities (see van Klinken et al 2021: 154–155; Burke 2014: 307–309). There is, then, a case to be made that any attempt to ground gender and heteronormativity in appeals to biblical literature may 'prove to be less secure, less "straight"-forward, or less inevitable than many of those who make such appeals imagine' (Stone 2011: 95). *The Queer Bible Commentary* is testimony to this (Guest et al, eds. 2006), as is Guest's compelling argument for genderqueering in Judges (Guest 2011).

36 Such assessment is now also expounded by former complementarians, notably Byrd (2020) and Barr (2021). Barr has left complementarian church after living within it for over forty years. Like Byrd, too, she remains Christian. Based on both her lived experience and her scholarship, primarily in Medieval History, Barr argues that

complementarian theology is 'wrong' and that it defends 'an interpretation that has been corrupted by our sinful human drive to dominate others and build hierarchies of power and oppression' (Barr 2021: 6–7). She professes that remaining silent has allowed 'both misogyny and abuse to run rampant in the church' (Barr 2021: 8).

37 Ortlund gets a bit carried away, describing Eve as 'perfectly gorgeous and uniquely suited to the man's need' (Ortlund 2006: 101). This statement imagines Eve as beautiful and her beauty as meeting a man's 'need'. The implication seems to be that the man's 'need' is for sex, aesthetic and sexual gratification, or attraction, and that the woman's purpose is to fulfil these. On the problematic potential of expectations of female beauty in evangelical contexts, see the preliminary work of Gretton-Dann (2021). Morse explains how 'primarily bodily language, emphasizing [Eve's] physical beauty' has been promoted by John Milton's 'most famous modern rewriting of Genesis' (Morse 2020: 43). Milton, too, Morse explains, while (like complementarians) 'keen to champion the mutual love of marriage... was also unable to view Adam and Eve as equals' (Morse 2020: 43).

38 As Thatcher pointed out in a presentation at the Modern Church conference (2022), creating 'male *and* female' cannot be equated with '*either* male *or* female (and nothing else)'.

39 There are, of course, plenty of feminist readings of the Adam and Eve story. One early, notable, and influential example, which identifies Eve's initiative and curiosity, and challenges the notion that male headship is a divinely mandated ideal, instead of a lamentable consequence of disobedience, is by Trible (1978: 72–143).

40 Eve is determinedly interpreted in RBMW as (only) Adam's wife. Eve can and has been interpreted also as Adam's daughter (born of his flesh), sister (with God being their father), and mother (with recourse to the possibility of an earlier story stratum). For details see Stiebert (2016: 136–138 and 152–154).

41 Elliot (RBMW 2006: 394–399) also sees the story of Adam and Eve as foundational for gender relations. She deems Eve 'calculating and self-serving' and contrasts this with Mary's complete and willing surrender. It is unclear how these motivations are derived from the sparse biblical text. Elliot continues that Mary's surrender is 'true mother-spirit, true maternity, so absent, it seems to me in all the annals of feminism' (Elliot 2006: 395). Morse explains how Eve, 'contrary to her biblical title as mother of all living' became 'cause of death', with Mary upstaging her. This occurred, Morse demonstrates, through the influence of such figures as Justin Martyr and Irenaeus of Lyons, not through close reading of the biblical text (Morse 2020: 49). For rabbinic parallels, see Thiede (forthcoming 2023).

42 On elective abortion and the Bible, see Stiebert (2022a).

43 This biblical verse and the verse following describe Miriam as a prophet and as singing and carrying a musical instrument, with the women following her. In the Hebrew Masoretic Text of 15:21, the pronominal suffix with the preposition (translating as '(she chanted) for them') is, however, plural masculine. Her direct command 'sing!' is also masculine (not feminine) plural. This does not align well with RBMW. God's words (of rebuke) about prophets, addressed to Miriam and Aaron, suggest that Miriam was someone to whom God made himself known in visions and dreams (Num 12:6). The passage also suggests that Moses is a superior prophet to Miriam and every other prophet, too (cf. Deut 34:10–12), but not that Miriam's leadership – be it of women, or women and men – was wrongful in itself, on account of her sex, or otherwise. She (not Aaron) is punished for challenging Moses; both Miriam and Aaron are rebuked (Num 12).

44 Again, the authors are not always consistent in their arguments. Female primary school teachers, for example, *are* acceptable because, 'little boys do not relate to their women teachers as man to woman, [so] the leadership dynamic ordained by God is not injured' (Piper and Grudem, RBMW 2006: 74).

45 We have seen several words associating women with strength and power: alongside *chayil* and *'oz*, also *'ôn* (see p.10, note 22) and *'ezer* (Gen 1:28, note 27). Also notable is that in Gen 2:24 it is the man who cleaves to the woman (i.e., implying that the one clinging is weaker than the one being clung to).
46 RBMW acknowledges a translation of 'strength' (Patterson, RBMW 2006: 368) but does not mention the common associations the Hebrew word has with warfare and (male) warriors.
47 RBMW acknowledges the woman's accomplishments in business affairs (Piper, RBMW 2006: 42).
48 Hunter, among many other biblical commentators, proposes that the woman described here is 'a model for wisdom' rather than an actual wife (Hunter 2011: 8) and points to the numerous ways in which the poem alludes to the description of Woman Wisdom in the early chapters of Proverbs (e.g., 31:10 and 3:15 and 8:11; 31:11 and 3:5, etc.) (Hunter 2011: 8, n.14). He comments also on the 'vitality, influence, and God-given strength of the woman's leadership within marriage', which, he continues, 'reminds us that the picture is much more complex and nuanced than is implied in the kind of male-female relationships normative in so-called "traditional" marriage' (2011: 9). While the woman of the poem has been widely praised by feminists and womanists, notes of caution regarding her idealisation, and the possible negative impact of such idealisation on actual women, are also important to consider (see Tan 2018).
49 The implication is clear from the inverted commas and the manipulation of the text to fit the predetermined complementarian scheme that finding oneself or wanting a career is not desirable for biblical womanhood.
50 See Elizabeth Elliot (RBMW 2006: 394–399). Elliot claims that there is a unity in 'the arrangement of the universe and the full harmony and tone of Scripture' (Elliot 2006: 394), again equating nature and Bible.
51 The ongoing work of the Avisa Project maps the history of sexual harassment and shows its reach far into the past (with particular emphasis on the European Middle Ages and Renaissance) and the entanglement with religious persons and institutions (see https://avisa.huma-num.fr/s/avisa-english/page/home).
52 Ortlund adds piously, 'I do not charge that [evangelical feminists] do so consciously. God alone knows our secret thoughts' (RBMW 2006: 111).
53 In his account of gendered and complementary roles, where males should lead, and females should submit, Piper refers to several examples of (mostly high-prestige) jobs deemed off-limits for women, because they 'stretch appropriate expressions of femininity beyond the breaking point' (Piper 2006: 50). Piper's recommendation is that women 'make God's business prosper' (Piper and Grudem 2006: 60). For married women this includes supporting their husbands and taking the primary caregiving role for any children. Having children, meanwhile, is, particularly for Köstenberger, the fulfilment of a divine command (Köstenberger 2011: 10). Women's work in the home, neighbourhood, or church (albeit not in leadership roles) is raised up as preferable to 'secular' employment (Piper and Grudem, RBMW 2006: 60). Such work, however, is also likely to be low-paid, or unpaid. The upshot of this for any women who do not find fulfilment in their 'Christ-desired' roles is potentially grave. In the real world, divorce rates among Christians are, as in the wider population, high and rising (see Pew Forum). Divorced women, divorced single mothers, like single mothers more generally, particularly if they have had no career, or no career in any well-paying sector, are highly likely to be particularly socio-economically vulnerable. The life mapped out by RBMW and Köstenberger indeed favours, even presumes, capitalism and some degree of economic prosperity where one parent (read: the mother) can (or should) stay home with (ideally multiple) children. Such is not viable for very many people, many of whom cite financial

constraints for postponing or for not having children (Stahl 2020). The complementarian scheme of RBMW would indeed make it difficult on multiple fronts, including financially, for a woman to leave an unhappy, or violent marriage, as well as to secure employment that can enable independent living.

54 Ortlund's generosity of accepting diversity as God-willed does not extend to gender diversity or non-heteronormative sexualities. A similar logic to Ortlund's (of accepting what is, because it is God-willed) is used with a different conclusion by Keeya, a pastor and one of the Ugandan LGBTQ+ refugees whose life-stories are featured in van Klinken et al (2021: 113–119). Keeya states 'it wasn't me who created myself, and no one taught [homosexuality] to me… it's God… God doesn't make mistakes' (2021: 113, 116).

55 Blyth (2021) shows how Bibles targeting teen girls effectively groom them in ways that enforce passivity and vulnerability to coercive control. Byrd (2020) and Barr (2021) write of their own and others' experiences of harm within complementarian churches.

56 On abuse and LLF, see Stiebert (2023). Thatcher argues that LLF minimises anything that 'would destroy the cosy (and plain wrong) assumption that "a clear biblical picture of marriage emerges when you consider Scripture as a whole, and in particular when you read it in the light of the teaching of Jesus on marriage" [LLF 281]'. Thatcher points out that there are forty-seven biblical references in a text box on Jesus and marriage extending over four pages but that, tellingly, Luke 20:34–35, which is negative on marriage, receives no mention.

57 Hobbs illustrates how these attitudes are propelled in sermons on divorce, which also describe divorce but not spousal abuse as 'tearing apart', 'breaking', violating, destroying, and even driving persons to kill themselves (Hobbs 2020: 315).

58 On dispelling claims that feminists are wrong and women are as violent as men, see Johnson (2005). On the predominance of domestic abuse being perpetrated by men, which is widely attested, see Dobash and Dobash (1979); Johnson (2015); and ONS (2020). There are also Christian sources testifying to this, such as Brown (2009); Everhart (2020); Paynter (2020); Clough (2022); and Koepping (2022).

59 This kind of 'logic' is far from uncommon. I have paraphrased here from Umberto Eco's summary of the 'argument' that purports to justify the authenticity of The Protocols of the Elders of Zion, in spite of irrefutable proof of their origin in a pastiche of plagiarised sources and falsehoods (Eisner 2006).

2 Marriage in the Bible

In this chapter, we will look more closely at how marriage is depicted *in the Bible*. We will demonstrate that much is inconclusive, and that what *is* clear is a widespread association in the Bible between marriage and violence. We will also examine the early Genesis chapters, Ephesians 5:21–33, and Malachi 2, because all these pericopes are often referred to as foundational or preeminent marriage proof-texts (e.g., Ortlund, in RBMW 2006: 95; Köstenberger 2011: 12). But first, we will look briefly at the notion of fixity in the Bible. As already stated, we do *not* feel bound by the Bible in the sense of 'what the Bible says, goes' but we want to illustrate why, even on the Bible's own terms, fixity is questionable and open to challenge. Indeed, a case can be made that any rigid adherence to 'what the Bible says' is negated by what the Bible itself recommends. (We have already mentioned and will again return to whether the Bible *says anything* at the end of this chapter.)

Fixity

In Matthew 5, Jesus is depicted as saying that he has come not to abolish but to fulfil the law and prophets. In the NRSV translation, the text continues with '…until heaven and earth pass away, not one letter, not one stroke of a letter, will pass from the law until all is accomplished' (Mt 5:18). Jesus appears to be stating that sacred texts – Law (Torah, or Pentateuch) and Prophets (or Nevi'im) – are first, prophetic, awaiting fulfilment, and second, written down with precision, down to the finest detail. Down to the iota (in the Koine Greek version), or to the last 'one jot or one tittle' (in the KJV translation), the sacred text will be accomplished. Does this also mean that no jot and tittle must ever be altered (cf. Deut 4:2; Prov 30:6)? As Jesus continues, it emerges that his interpretation extrapolates from and elaborates on the sacred text. Prohibition of murder is extended to include prohibition of feelings of anger towards another (Mt 5:21–24); prohibition of adultery is extended to include looking at a woman with lust (Mt 5:27–28)[1]; divorce and taking an oath, which are permitted in the Law, are condemned (Mt 5:31–37); and the law of Exodus 21:24a is quoted and then inverted (Mt 5:38–42). Jesus's words both affirm biblical

DOI: 10.4324/9781003152668-3

law but also subvert it in the process of interpretation. The ancient law may be unchanged, down to jot and tittle, but it holds different meaning for Jesus; the text may be fixed but how it is read changes.

Contrary to Köstenberger's claim (Köstenberger 2011: 20, see above), biblical text is constantly renegotiated and revised. This is what the gospel text describes Jesus as doing: renegotiating and revising. Divorce may or may not have been easy or common, but there was provision for and mention of it in Law (Deut 24:1–3) and Prophets (Isa 50:1; Jer 3:8).[2] A man could not remarry a woman who had, upon divorce from him, married and divorced someone else; but otherwise, remarriage for divorced persons appears to have been legal (Deut 24:4; cf. Jer 3:1). But Jesus renegotiates and revises this; now, with few exceptions, remarriage constitutes adultery (Mt 5:32); and adultery results not only from a sexual act but also from a lustful desire (Mt 5:28).

It has been proposed that Jesus's motivation here is to protect women, who may have been rendered particularly vulnerable by divorce and the loss of protection and reputation that followed in its wake. As Mary Rose D'Angelo points out, however, this is difficult to ascertain. While there might be a case to be made for Jesus as a champion for women, in the Greek Bible '[g]ender roles and marriage have been mutually defining' and much about both is left unsaid. Ultimately, D'Angelo is correct, 'both divorce and its unavailability' could be said to disadvantage women. Any evidence for liberationist motivation, consequently, is at best ambiguous (D'Angelo 2014: 500) – not least because, as Meredith Warren has pointed out, the popular 'perception of Jesus as friend of women' requires serious interrogation (Warren 2022: 218). For example, Warren notes how Jesus shames the Samaritan woman at the well (John 4) by referring to her five husbands. Moreover, by continuing to read the story uncritically in terms of Jesus fraternising 'even' with a woman of such dubious reputation, serves to perpetuate rape culture attitudes.

Supporters of complementarian ideology, as we have seen, emphasise and spin select biblical verses in particular ways. They do not admit to peddling their ideology but instead claim to be interpreting sacred text as intended, or to be distilling out the 'true' meaning. While we cannot know whether the Scripture Jesus is depicted as referring to, and quoting from, is the same as that canonised now in the Jewish Tanakh and Christian Old Testament, it has indeed been fixed now for centuries.[3] And yet, for all this, it continues to be variously interpreted, with different features foregrounded as times and preoccupations change.

While some Christian supersessionist rhetoric depicts Judaism as stuck in time and clinging on to 'old' laws, post-biblical Rabbinic Judaism shows plenty of evidence against such fixity. The Talmud's *Bava Metzia* (30b) advocates against being restricted by law and for going beyond the letter of law, and the discussions between the Tannaitic schools of Hillel and Shammai are often focused on whether to stick firmly to the law as written down (Shammai), or to an interpretation more lenient and tolerant (Hillel). Most often, it is the school of Hillel that determines halakhah (normative Jewish law).

We mention this to show that fixity, the idea of a God-ordained permanent truth imparted at the time of creation of humans, or some time thereafter, and as recorded in 'the Bible' and then faithfully performed ever after, could itself be considered unbiblical. Not only are there many other examples in the Christian Bible, of the Greek Bible renegotiating and revising the Hebrew Bible – such as, regarding the role of Abraham and Sarah (Gal 3–4), or the covenant of male circumcision (Rom 3–8) – there are references within the Hebrew Bible of changes over time. A portion of the Ten Commandments – one of the most famous and cherished texts of the entire Bible – is renegotiated and revised. Hence, it says, 'for I the LORD your God am a jealous God, punishing children for the iniquity of parents, to the third and the fourth generation of those who reject me, but showing steadfast love to the thousandth generation of those who love me and keep my commandments' (Exod 20:5–6). But later, this is rejected, and each person will bear their own sin, not any inherited iniquity (Jer 31:29–30; Ezek 18:1–20). By the Bible's own account, God changes his mind, including about significant matters, like the destruction of Nineveh and its more than 120,000 citizens and numerous animals (Jonah 3:10; 4:11); God makes new covenants that overhaul previous ones (Jer 31:31); and God does evil and makes amends later (Job 42:11–12). Indeed, written down laws that are rigidly followed no matter what, even when they could lead to injustice, are mocked. This applies to the Greek Bible's characterisation of the Pharisees as sticklers for the law, as well as to the depiction of the immovable laws of the Persians (Daniel 6; Book of Esther)[4] as ludicrous.

> For the past years for International Women's Day and the 16 Days of Activism, I've been working with activists in Kenya. I've learned from them that Kenya's Marriage Act (2014) prohibits marital union that is not voluntary and consenting, and that the legal age of marriage is 18 and above. I've also learned from them that up to one in four marriages in northern Kenya especially involves a girl under age 18 – sometimes as young as 11.[5] This is not a problem confined to Kenya – which is also, incidentally, 85%+ Christian. I see something comparable here in the UK, including in my community of Blackburn: that good laws don't prevent bad things happening and that religious law and custom can exert strong force – strong enough to resist the law and risk criminality. Where marriage is concerned this has horrendous and profound impact – impact that is personal and intergenerational and seeps through whole communities.
>
> (Saima)

The notion of a law ossified in the Bible, and of insistence on its rigid enforcement through time – as proposed (albeit selectively) in the arguments of biblical marriage – flies in the face of how language, social mores, perceptions, and laws change over time as testified within the Bible itself.[6] The Bible can be read as a diverse record of significant (or, using religious language, inspired) words from ancient times but is best thought of as a library, rather than a book. Since its canonisation, and throughout changing times, some biblical passages come to the fore or recede, depending on the preoccupations of successive eras.[7]

In our present, with the social fault line that is 'the pink line', biblical texts are used in public forums both to reject and to accommodate same-sex love, marriage, and adoption.[8] In terms of accommodation, this can be justified as an example of renegotiation: in times where gender and sexual orientation are better understood, same-sex marriage, marriage involving non-binary persons, and polyamorous marriage can have legitimacy alongside the traditional 'one man and one woman' marriage, which became the norm over against polygynous marriage, evidenced in some layers of the Bible. In some settings, such a suggestion is bound to elicit the horrified response and accusation of removing *all* restrictions and opening the way for incestuous, child-, bestial, or forced 'marriage'. In this vein, Republican Representative Louie Gohmert, to give one of multiple examples, stated that when one seeks to redefine 'marriage' as not being only between one man and one woman, 'then why not have three men and one woman or four women and one man? …Or why not, you know, somebody has a love for an animal or -? There is no clear place to draw a line once you eliminate the traditional marriage' (Parnass 2013). Again, this betrays a kind of hysterical alarmism we have already encountered: the notion that *any* modification of biblical marriage will unleash chaos and ruination.

But renegotiating the meaning of marriage does not have to mean 'anything goes'. Marriage and marriage law have, indeed, been renegotiated in multiple ways over time and even many very conservative Christians have no problem with many of these changes. Notably, certainly in our setting, legal changes include that women are not treated as chattel, that consent to marriage is a requirement, and that there is a minimum marital age.[9] On 27 February 2023, the Marriage and Civil Partnership (Minimum Age) Act 2022 came into effect, raising the age of marriage and civil partnership in England and Wales from age 16 (with parental permission) to age 18. Again, this change in law reflects changing societal attitudes and increased awareness of the possibility of 16- and 17-year-olds being coerced into marriage.[10] Laws change – often for good reason – and chaos need not ensue. This does not equate for us to advocacy of 'anything goes'. Consenting same-sex marriage between two adult persons does not violate or limit anyone else's rights. Prohibiting it, however, does.[11]

At present, it is the pink line that is especially prominent and divisive. Other topics have risen to prominence in other times: the humanity or deity of Jesus, the nature and role of the Holy Spirit, the acceptance or rejection of enslavement, intermarriage and miscegenation, and ordination of women, to name just a few.[12] Again and again, the library of the Bible can be and has been used to build the argument on either side of a polemic, testifying to its range of content. Next, we will look at what the Bible says about marriage, including content that does not tend to appear in 'biblical marriage' constructions.

Marriage in the Bible: A Mixed Picture

Important to mention at the outset is that there is very little description of either weddings or marriages in the Bible overall.[13] Evidence of any ritual or ceremony, for instance, is scattered and mostly inconclusive. Pertinent vocabulary, too, is sparse. There is no Hebrew word that neatly maps on to either the English word 'marriage' or the word 'divorce'.[14] There is only one Hebrew word (*'ishshâ*), and one Greek word (*gunē*), and each translates into English as both 'adult female/woman' and 'wife'. The Hebrew word for 'adult male/man' is *'îsh*, and the Greek *anēr*, both of which are also sometimes translated 'husband', as is a second Hebrew word *ba'al*, sometimes meaning 'owner' or 'lord'.[15] As can be inferred from this dual meaning of *ba'al*, the perspective and worldview of much of the Bible assumes or confers male authority, with women or wives sometimes depicted as chattel or economic commodities.[16]

Indeed, one predominant set of contexts for marriage in the Bible is blatantly transactional. Some references make it clear that marriage entails payment of some kind to the prospective wife's father. Hence, negotiations between fathers over Dinah include discussion of a wedding present, or bridewealth, or fine, to be received by Jacob, Dinah's father (Gen 34:12)[17]; while David 'earns' Michal with the bride price or dowry of Philistine foreskins demanded by Saul (1 Sam 18:25), and Jacob pays with 14 years of labour for marriages to Laban's daughters, Leah and Rachel (Gen 29:18–30). Other times, a payment is made by the father of the bride: hence, Pharaoh gives the conquered and ransacked habitation of Gezer to his daughter, who marries Solomon (1 Kgs 9:16–17). (It is Solomon, not Pharaoh's daughter, who builds in Gezer, indicating that the payment is, effectively, for Solomon.)[18] The purpose of marriage is not transparent in Hosea 3:1–2, whereas it is earlier (Hos 1:2–3). In the wider metaphor of which it is a part (Hos 1–3), these verses state that a woman can be bought for the purpose of 'love' (from *'ahaḇ*).[19] Certainly, enslaved women are elsewhere depicted as a man's property, and as sexually available (married?) to him (e.g., Deut 21:10–13),[20] with any violations of another *man's* rights concerning such women relatively easily sorted out (Lev 19:20–22). The women have no rights.

Transactional attitudes to what may be marriage are also evident in the way girls and women are a reward, or spoils, of war (Num 31:18; Deut 21:10–14),[21] as well as in how the inheritance of the brotherless daughters of Zelophehad preserves men's property rights through marriage within the paternal clan (i.e., cousin marriage, Num 36:1–12, see especially v.11).[22] One occasion when a man's wife is not ultimately his is when the man is enslaved: according to enslavement laws in Exodus, if an enslaved man is given a wife by his master (*'adon*) and she bears sons or daughters, then, if the man 'chooses' in his seventh year of enslavement to leave, he must leave behind his wife and children (21:2–4). The woman in such a case is doubly owned – by her husband *and* by the man who 'owns' him. Ultimately, she and her children are the master's, and, given multiple biblical narratives that demonstrate how men sexually access enslaved women, it is likely that the master asserted sexual access to her and that she had no recourse to anything resembling autonomy or consent.[23]

David Clines, in his study of the language of violence, points out how androcentrism and reification of women are evident in marriage vocabulary: 'The terms "to take *[lqch]* a woman" and "to give *[ntn]* a woman" (still astonishingly used in our own culture) mean no more than the transfer of a woman from the authority of her father to that of her husband (with the additional imposition of sexual services).[24] To call this "marriage" can only be a euphemism'. He adds, 'I do not deny that in ancient Israel there was mutual desire and mutual sexual activity. I am just registering the fact that there is no language expressing mutuality' (Clines 2020: 17–18, online version). Alastair Hunter adds two more marriage verbs: *nasa'* (literally, 'to lift up')[25] and *'aras* ('to betroth'), the latter expressing, rather like *lqch* a man's 'wish to have a particular woman' (Hunter 2011: 14).[26] The former has only male subjects[27] and Hunter, too, rather like Clines, concedes that 'patriarchal attitudes and sexist assumptions' suffuse the biblical text (Hunter 2011: 2), particularly the legal corpus, which is composed 'firmly in the context of a male point of view' (Hunter 2011: 5).[28] Both commentators stress that both the shortage and the bias of depictions need to be kept in mind in any discussion of marriage and the Bible.

It is clear: marriage in the Bible covers some (rather imprecisely depicted) practices whereby men take or purchase women. Moreover, a man having sex with, inclusive of raping, a woman appears sometimes to be equivalent with marriage. Such practices, thankfully, are neither advocated in biblical marriage ideologies nor would they be dignified with the designation 'marriage' in our context. Still, they are there. In the Bible. We will shortly explore more closely the multiple connections between marriage and violence in the Bible. In the ensuing chapter, we will develop why doing so matters. Before we establish these connections, and then move on to focus briefly on three key biblical texts widely drawn on to solidify the case for 'biblical marriage' and against divorce (namely, Genesis 1–3, Ephesians 5, and Malachi 2), we will first draw attention to some of the arguably positive depictions of, or associations with, marriage.

Positive Depictions – With Some Caveats

It is wrong to say that violence is a constant feature of weddings or marriages in the Bible. Alastair Hunter's full analysis of marriage in the Hebrew Bible makes this clear,[29] as do the chapters on marriage and divorce covering both testaments and the ancient Near East more generally in *The Oxford Encyclopedia of the Bible and Gender Studies* (2014).

Courtship is rarely mentioned in the Bible, but Annalisa Azzoni proposes that a man might occasionally have had some input regarding his choice of bride, 'as attested in the narratives where a smitten son [Shechem or Samson] asks his parents to give him a specific woman as wife (Gen 34; Judg 14:2)' (Azzoni 2014: 485). Admittedly, there is no mention here of the women's stand.[30] The sole Hebrew Bible example where the verb *'ahab* (most often translated 'to love')[31] has a female subject and male object refers to Michal's feeling for David prior to their marriage (1 Sam 18:20, 28).[32] In keeping with aforementioned androcentrism and male dominance, actions of love, sex, or marriage almost exclusively have male, not female, subjects.[33]

There is not a great deal of pre- or peri-marital romance, with the possible (if unlikely) exception of the anomalous Song of Songs, which celebrates erotic love. Hunter argues for 'a frankness about, and celebration of the sheer sexual pleasure to be found in human relationships', citing both Song of Songs and Proverbs 5:18–19. He is cautious, however, not to claim that Song of Songs is about eroticism *in marriage*. Indeed, only when one starts with the assumption that sex is acceptable exclusively in heterosexual marriage, and that therefore the Song of Songs, being in the Bible, must *ipso facto* be about a married couple, can one refer to this book as 'the Bible's one book about marital love and romance' (Ortlund 2023).[34]

When this assumption is suspended, there is actually much in the text to contradict, or make uncertain, any assertion of a marital union. Yes, there is mention of a betrothal or wedding day (Song 3:11); and yes, the beloved is called a 'bride' (though also a 'sister') (e.g., Song 4:9–12)[35]; but the lovers are also barred from each other: 'A garden locked… a fountain sealed' (Song 4:12). Moreover, the lovers in the text seem to be running around in the countryside (Song 2:8; 6:1–2), and even by night on urban streets (Song 3:1–2; 5:7) trying to find each other. They wish to be together but cannot: they are despised if they kiss (Song 8:1), and brothers seem to guard their sister to obstruct her lover's advances (Song 8:8–9). None of this sounds like married life. As Phyllis Trible puts it, 'Never is this woman called a wife, nor is she required to bear children. In fact, to the issue of marriage and procreation the Song does not speak' (Trible 1978: 162). The Song might conceivably be some kind of romantic wedding drama but in its detail, it is hardly descriptive of marital lovemaking and more of youthful fantasy.[36]

Hunter finds the 'openness and honesty', as well as the 'frankness about, and celebration of … sheer sexual pleasure' in the Song 'refreshing', adding also the 'naïve charm of Proverbs 5:18–19', which celebrates the woman, or wife, of one's youth (Hunter 2011: 8). Following up on this 'companion (or partner) of one's youth', a figure mentioned, or possibly alluded to, a number of times in biblical literature (Isa 54:6; Jer 2:2; 3:4; Ezek 16:60; Joel 1:8; Mal 2:14, 15; Prov 2:17; 5:18), Hunter speculates about 'betrothal at an early age', possibly 'pre-pubertal betrothal' (Hunter 2011: 12). This is viewed by Hunter in wistfully nostalgic terms (cf. Hos 2:15, Heb 2:17), with 'the possibility that such a youthful partner … [was] a friend or companion as well as husband or wife' (Hunter 2011: 26). While he admits that it is impossible to draw 'any firm conclusion', he points to early betrothal being a custom 'common in many pre-modern societies' (Hunter 2011: 12).[37]

Often marriages in the Bible are depicted as arranged by parents (Gen 27:46–28:2), by the father (Gen 38:6), or the father through a trusted mediator (Gen 24), and occasionally by the mother (Gen 21:21).[38] Rebekah is asked and assents to marriage to Isaac, sight unseen (Gen 24:58). She and her family members receive costly gifts (Gen 24:53), and she goes to Isaac attended by a companion, maids, and blessing (Gen 24:59–61).

It is fair to say that some cases can be made for marital love, loyalty, and desire. If Genesis 2–3 is read as a text that describes marriage (of which more below), we see here the man's delight in and celebration of the woman (Gen 2:23),[39] and the statement that a man will leave his parents and cleave[40] to his woman, or wife (Gen 2:24). Moreover, one could say the woman's (sexual?) desire for her man, or husband, is divinely mandated (Gen 3:16, cf. Morse 2020: 24),[41] and Sarah also speaks of 'pleasure'[42] in a passage that clearly alludes to procreative sex with Abraham, her husband (Gen 18:12). It says of Isaac that he loved Rebekah and that she comforted him after his mother, Sarah's, death (Gen 24:67), as well as that he does something to Rebekah (translated 'fondling' in NRSV),[43] which causes Abimelech to conclude that she is Isaac's wife, not sister (Gen 26:8–9). Elkanah, too, loves his wife Hannah (1 Sam 1:5), asking her if he is not better to her than tens sons (1 Sam 1:8).[44] Finding a wife is occasionally equated with something good and with divine favour (Prov 18:22; 19:14).[45] Ananias and Sapphira, while ultimately rebuked and punished for their collusion, are a married couple who act together and are buried together (Acts 5:1–10).

Weddings are not described in any detail in the Bible. Anything that can be said about them has to be cobbled together from scattered allusions. If Psalm 45 is an epithalamion (wedding song) then the implication is that weddings – certainly royal weddings – were lavish celebrations, involving fanfare and multiple attendants (Ps 45:9, 14, Heb 45:10, 15), as well as music, gifts, and magnificent robes (Ps 45:8, 12–14, Heb 45:9, 13–15).[46] Royal weddings may well have been aimed at forging, or cementing, alliances or loyalties. This is most clear when Solomon marries the daughter of Pharaoh (the verb used here is from *ch-t-n*, 1 Kgs 3:1).[47] There is mention of feasting on the occasion of what appears to be the formalising of a union, such as that of Jacob and Leah (Gen 29:22, though, of course, Jacob thought he was marrying her sister, Rachel; cf. Judg 14:10).[48] Elsewhere – such as when David 'takes' Ahinoam (1 Sam 25:43), or Abigail and Bathsheba 'become' his wives (1 Sam 25:42; 2 Sam 11:27), there is no mention of any ritual or ceremony.[49] There are some indistinct poetic references to what might be a wedding ritual (Joel 2:16; Ps 19:5), as well as mentions of ornate garments and jewellery (Isa 49:18; 61:10; Jer 2:32; Ezek 16:10–13) and of anointing (Ezek 16:9; Ps 45:7, Heb 45:8). But a marriage contract (*ketubah*), signed before witnesses alongside a blessing does not appear anywhere until the book of Tobit (7:6, cf. Sefaria).[50]

Wedding and marriage metaphors appear multiple times in the Bible. Restoration in Isaiah is described as a move away from desolation towards delight and is depicted in terms of marriage motifs where the land is taken back by God (Isa 62:4–5). This is conveyed through words of marriage that signify mastery or rule (*b'l*). In Hosea, on the other hand, a term from this root, *ba'ali*, 'my master', is contrasted with the preferred *'îshî*, 'my husband' (Hos 2:16, Heb 2:18). *Ba'ali*, moreover, is associated with the similar-sounding word for foreign gods (*ba'alim*, Hos 2:17, Heb 2:19). Marriage metaphors in prophetic texts are shocking in that they describe a wife abandoning her husband for other lovers, which signifies Israel's deplorable abandonment of God for other gods (Hos 1–3; Jer 3:1–5; Ezek 16 and 23). But shocking, too, as we will go on to discuss, is the violent punishment God exacts.

In the Greek Bible wedding (*gamos*) imagery is used metaphorically to depict Christ as bridegroom or husband and a community as bride or wife (e.g., 2 Cor 11:2).[51] Another usage conveys a mood of festivity and joyfulness. The wedding of Cana is an occasion for gathering, celebrating, and making merry with wine (Jn 2:1–10). Metaphorically, the ministry of Jesus is identified with the happy time when a groom is with his companions, celebrating (Mk 2:19; Mt 9:15; Lk 5:34), and the kingdom of heaven is likened in Jesus's parables to a wedding feast (Mt 22:2) and the arrival of the bridegroom (Mt 25:10). The two are also frequently combined. Hence, in Revelation the eschatological future is depicted as the wedding of personified New Jerusalem, the bride, to Jesus, the Lamb (Rev 19:7; 21:2; cf. 22:17). This is depicted as a celebration, with rejoicing and splendid garments (Rev 19:6–8). A consistent element, as D'Angelo points out, is subordination of the metaphorical or actual female to the metaphorical or actual male (D'Angelo 2014: 501).

The motif of covenant (*berit*), particularly in Hosea (e.g., Hos 2:18, Heb 2:20), has drawn interest from some theologians who interpret covenant as conveying something about the sacrosanct status of marriage. Hence, Köstenberger characterises marriage as 'a divine, not merely human, institution…, based on God's design and sovereign plan… whose permanence is safeguarded by none other than God himself' (Köstenberger 2011: 4–5). This plan prescribes permanence, sacredness, intimacy, mutuality (which, he stresses, is not sameness) and exclusiveness (Köstenberger 2011:5–8). Hunter, however, points out with regard to Hosea 1–3 that there exist 'complexities and moral ambivalence' in the text, leading him to feel uncertain whether the chapters describe 'an uplifting example of persistent love, or a sexist tract devoted to the denigration of women' (Hunter 2011: 11). There is nothing as precise or definite as Köstenberger's description of a covenant of marriage.[52] Hunter concedes, however, that there is significance in the metaphorical association between breach of covenant between God and Israel and the ending of a marriage: 'not because marriage depended on a covenant, but because the intensity of the divine-human bond can only adequately be described using terms associated with the closest forms of human-to-human relationships'

(Hunter 2011: 31).⁵³ He adds that 'the one clear context in which the covenant is a human emotional bond' pertains not to a man and a woman, but to David and Jonathan, two men (1 Sam 18:1–3).⁵⁴

Hunter's approach is one he describes as going 'back to the source' (Hunter 2011: 3). His thorough review of marriage terms, themes, and mentions, while not disguising that the Hebrew Bible contains material that describes or implies negative consequences, especially for women (e.g., Hunter 2011: 10–14), sees some basis for positive lessons and influences in the present. He sees evidence for celebrating sexuality (Hunter 2011: 8), and for strong praiseworthy emotions, including within marriage and family life (Hunter 2011: 27–29). Hunter argues for precedents for companionable pair bonding, in the companion of youth motif; for celebrating women's 'leadership within marriage', on the basis of Proverbs 31:10–35 (Hunter 2011: 9); and for wives and mothers being 'a powerful source of prosperity at the very centre of everything the household stands for', on the basis of Psalm 128 (Hunter 2011: 9). Hunter also points out that some 'irregular relationships' (such as those of Judah and Tamar in Genesis 38, or Ruth and Boaz in the Book of Ruth) do not seem to present any insurmountable problems, indicating welcome flexibility and accommodation (Hunter 2011: 6). Hunter considers most of the legal matters concerning marriage (e.g., levirate marriage) to be no longer of relevance, and, for all 'the bitter rhetoric against [intermarriage]', he chooses not to discuss it at any length, because 'it is an uncontroversial issue in the contemporary church' (Hunter 2011: 27). Hunter is open to accommodating divorce, seeing no compelling evidence for opposition to it, and is cautiously open to same-sex marriage, stating, that his 'social and cultural instincts are to go down the road of "complementary pairs" in a more extended sense' than heteronormative pairing (Hunter 2011: 30).

Next, we will discuss how positive depictions of marriage are overcast by an abundance of associations between marriage and violence.

Negative Depictions

We have already mentioned that any understanding of 'marriage in the Bible' is complicated by the diversity of vocabulary (with no Hebrew word capturing *gamos* or 'marriage'), by gaps in knowledge, and by how scattered allusions to marriage are. What emerges from the Bible is no neat and coherent picture or definition of marriage. We challenge the narrow construction of biblical marriage that complementarian interpreters extract from the Bible. Some of the examples of marriage are ambiguous, even questionable. Does Proverbs 31:10–31 really refer to an actual admired wife, or Song of Songs to joyful sex in marriage, or Hosea to a forbearing husband doing all he can to save his marriage? We see good reason for doubt. Still, we have found and discussed some biblical passages that indeed allude to inter-human bonding and affection, and these may indeed reflect and celebrate some marital relationships, too.[55] But just as it would be wrong to deny or ignore these positive glimpses, it is also wrong to deny or ignore the multiple biblical passages that associate marriage with violence.

Numbers 5:11–31 is one of the lengthiest legal texts relating to marriage in the Hebrew Bible – and a text complementarian interpreters ignore. Indeed, this text is very widely ignored in Christian settings. Given its violence, we hardly advocate for using it as a model for marriage. Its references to the tabernacle and association with magical rituals render it irrelevant in our time. The tabernacle is the forerunner of the temple – and there is not even a temple in Jerusalem any longer. Hence, the sacrifices described in this pericope (5:15, 18, 25–26) are no longer a requirement, even in orthodox forms of Judaism. Moreover, the seemingly magical properties of 'the water of bitterness that brings the curse' (5:18, 24) make this text particularly bizarre to modern ears. Still, unlike some other texts selected and drawn into instruction-giving on marriage (like Genesis 1–3, which we shall go on to discuss), Numbers 5 is clearly about a married couple.

The law in Numbers 5 describes the scenario of what a man is to do if he feels jealous because his wife 'goes astray' and 'is unfaithful to him' (5:12, NRSV) but without his having any proof. There follows a lengthy description of a disturbing and shaming ritual. As part of this, the woman is brought to the tabernacle before the priest, where her hair is dishevelled, and she is made to drink a potion that will reveal either her guilt or her innocence. Indeed, whereas her guilt is first assumed (5:12–13) it is later thrown into some degree of doubt (5:14). Not only may she be wholly innocent, but the person with whom she *might* have 'gone astray' is not deemed co-responsible[56] or 'defiled', whereas she is (5:14). There is no indication in this text that the woman has any defence or agency: instead, she has things done to her and her only utterance is words of submission, 'Amen. Amen' (5:22).[57] Moreover, the jealous husband is completely exonerated of all blame (5:31), even if the woman is found blameless. He appears to have the right to accuse her, without any evidence, simply on account of his jealousy, because his wife is 'under his authority' (5:29).

This law does not appear in the complementarian texts to defend wives' submission and obedience to their husbands' headship we have examined – but it certainly depicts such submission, alongside promoting another complementarian marital value, namely sexual exclusiveness. Moving past the strange elements of divination, the husband's destructive jealousy on display here is not unfamiliar, right up to our present.[58] Disturbingly, this is not criticised – either in the biblical text or by the commentators on biblical marriage.[59] Here is a text about a marital crisis, precipitated by a husband's suspicion and possibly unfounded jealousy. It is also a text of tremendous violence: the violence of physically manoeuvring the woman (quite probably entirely against her will) into the tabernacle and subjecting her to the ritual; the violence of accusing the woman (possibly publicly) of illicit sex; the violence of making her drink an unpleasant potion; the violence of threatening her with miscarriage or infertility (which is described in graphic language); the possible consequence of miscarriage; and the violence, if she passes the ordeal, of continuing in marriage to a jealous and mistrustful man.[60]

This is no isolated example. Another casuistic law in Deuteronomy (22:13–30) describes another scenario, this time of a husband who accuses his newly-wed wife of not having been a virgin. This time a public proof of virginity is required (Deut 22:17). Whereas in Numbers 5, the emphasis is on the wife's guilt, with the possibility of her innocence something of an afterthought, and with the husband completely exonerated, Deuteronomy 22 is different. Here the initial assumption is that *the husband* is guilty of slander (Deut 22:14); in the event that proof of virginity is provided, he is fined, and cannot ever divorce his wife (Deut 22:19). The possibility of the wife's guilt is considered but is less prominent than the possibility of her innocence. However, as in Numbers 5, she is punished either way: if she is innocent, she is married for life to a man who dislikes her (Deut 22:13, 19); if she is guilty, she is stoned to death (Deut 22:21). In both laws, the woman's sexual continence is a subject of public speculation; and both scenarios cannot but cause women distress.[61]

In a whole host of other texts there is description of rape transpiring in marriage. Sarai taking 'Hagar the Egyptian, her slave-girl' and giving her 'to her husband Abram as a wife' (Gen 16:3), so that he will 'go in to' Hagar (16:2, 4) to produce a child for Sarai (16:2) would by today's standards amount to sexual exploitation, rape, and coercive surrogacy. Zanne Domoney-Lyttle has demonstrated that in the text and its translation into English, as well as in many visual depictions of Genesis 16:3–4, Sarai is presented as presiding over a 'marriage' between Hagar and Abram. Yet there is no trace of any ceremony in the text, and, by referring to Hagar as a 'wife'[62] a reader is encouraged to view the union as respectable, legal, consenting, sanctioned by God, and as legitimate 'rather than as a forced marriage between a slave and a powerful man for the purpose of producing Sarai's surrogate child' (2018). Shechem's rape of Dinah is a prelude to wedding negotiations (Gen 34:2–4, 8–12). Marriage without possibility of divorce is the proposed 'solution' for a raped un-betrothed virgin and her rapist (Deut 22:28).[63] This law seems to be confirmed by the story of Tamar, who is raped by her brother Amnon. Before the rape, Tamar pleads with Amnon to speak to the king, their father, implying that he would authorise their marriage (2 Sam 13:13). After the rape, she again pleads with him not to cast her out (2 Sam 13:16), suggesting that marriage is the one way to salvage her dignity and reputation.

Laura Robinson points out that marriage negotiations and weddings, while certainly 'causes for celebration' (Robinson 2022: 171) are frequently enmeshed with violence. She points, for instance, to David's brutish payment of Philistine foreskins (1 Sam 18:26–27) and to Othniel's capture of Keriath-Sepher (Judg 1:12–13) both in pursuit of brides: Michal and Achsah, respectively. She also points to the 'debacle' of Samson's wedding (Judg 14:10–15:6), which 'results in the violent exchange of clothes and the bride, and finally the deaths of most of the characters' (Robinson 2022: 174). Modern tendencies to link weddings with romantic and sentimental notions may obscure this but, she explains, '[a]ncient weddings were complex economic affairs requiring extensive prenuptial negotiations concerning property, money, and family. In literature and mythology, these negotiations often break down into violence, in which the bride is at once party to the proceedings and also a commodity over which other parties debate' (Robinson 2022: 169). This can make weddings particularly 'tense occasions in which hostile parties are forced into closer quarters, with the threat of violence and loss looming over the proceedings' (Robinson 2022: 170). Adjusting her focus to view weddings in terms of 'the exchange of power… including the bodies of human beings' (Robinson 2022: 170), Robinson re-evaluates wedding imagery in two parables of the gospel of Matthew (22:1–14; 25:1–13) and asks of these apocalyptic chapters, 'Why weddings?' (Robinson 2022: 170).

The answer is that because weddings involve 'such complete changes of allegiance… Matthew views them as mini-apocalypses' (Robinson 2022: 179). The first parable features recalcitrant persons who will not attend the wedding to which they are invited. Some seize, abuse, and kill the servants of the king making the invitation (22:6). The king retaliates violently, sending troops to kill the offenders and burn their city (22:7). More guests are invited but one who is not dressed for the occasion is bound and cast out (22:14). The second parable is less violent but features uncompromising exclusion of the five virgins who fail to prepare for the bridegroom's arrival. As Robinson explains, both wedding-themed parables stress first, 'divisions between guests' and second, 'the necessity of completely submitting oneself to the program of the groom' (Robinson 2022: 177). Another shared feature is that in both stories nothing can prevent the wedding banquet: 'However vigorously it may be fought, Israel's eschatological fufillment will occur… and no amount of resistance can prevent it' (Robinson 2022: 179). Robinson also points out concealed but assumed gendered violence. Hence, the bridegroom gets his way, no matter what. The bride, or her consent, is not of critical interest to the narrator, just as bridal consent is not of interest in multiple ancient sources, such as the bulk of Hebrew Bible narratives relevant to marriage. Robinson concludes from this that '[e]schatological victory for Matthew is violent and occurs in the context of marital domination' (Robinson 2022: 179), a domination that is not questioned.

Rape marriage is described also in contexts of war. In Numbers 31 Moses, acting on divine instruction (31:1–2) and as avenger for Israel's deity (31:16), orders that all males, including little boys, be killed, along with 'every woman who has known a man' (31:17). The only Midianites to be exempted from mass slaughter are 'young girls who have not known a man'; these girls are for the Israelites (31:18). The implication here, with the reference to the girls' virginity and to being 'for' the Israelites, is marriage, possibly child marriage.

Yet again, if we are prepared to call this 'marriage' we are applying the word to something acutely violent.[64]

Again, such 'marriage' is not a one-off. An Israelite soldier who sees among the captives a beautiful woman whom he desires and wants to marry (literally, 'take for [him]self for a wife/woman', a standard biblical expression translated with marriage terminology), can do so. Following a series of rituals and a waiting period, he can 'go in to her and be her husband (*ba'al*)' (Deut 21:11–13). If the husband is not pleased with her, he can let her go but not sell her – because he has raped her (21:14).[65] Again, using the term 'marriage' for this legal text needs to come with a warning. Barbara Thiede is correct that '[w]e might call what this text describes an arranged rape, but certainly not an arranged marriage' (2022b: 9). As she points out, to call this a 'marriage' is to give a free pass to rape by colluding with the biblical texts and 'excusing and rationalizing their violent content' (2022b: 9). As above, using the word 'marriage' (or related expressions, such as 'take for a wife') to translate certain biblical passages has to acknowledge the violence absorbed into the concept. The normalising upshot of such translation requires flagging up and calling out.

Rape marriage is once more depicted as a 'solution' in Judges 21. Here, where the posterity of the tribe of Benjamin is in jeopardy because other Israelite tribes have made a solemn oath not to give their daughters in marriage to a Benjaminite, virgin women are first seized from Jabesh-gilead while their families, all males and 'every woman that has lain with a male' are slaughtered (Judg 21:10–14). When there are still not enough women for the Benjaminites, yet more women are seized, this time from Shiloh (Judg 21:21). The seized women's relatives are advised to be 'generous' (Judg 21:22). There may be implicit criticism of this violence in that the chapter concludes with the comment that 'there was no king in Israel; all the people did what was right in their own eyes' (Judg 21:25) but there is nothing more explicit.

These examples of sexual abuse leading up to and transpiring in marriage are shocking. Violence *in* marriage is also in evidence in biblical texts. This is most notable in the prophetic marriage metaphor, and has been discussed at length by multiple feminist commentators, particularly with reference to Hosea 1–3 and Ezekiel 16 and 23.[66] In both prophetic books, an extended metaphor draws associations between, on the one hand, the disobedient and idolatrous Israelites who deserve the divine punishment coming their way, and, on the other, a husband and his disobedient, adulterous wife. In Hosea, the prophet is told to take a deviant wife, Gomer, who will go after her lovers and be punished with confinement and shameful exposure before being taken back. This is cast as an analogy of God's relationship with idolatrous Israel. The violent punishment of Gomer, then, is depicted as justified and sanctioned by God. Feminist commentators have pointed out that, much like the legitimation of the husband's jealousy in Numbers 5, marital abuse is here legitimated. Ezekiel 16 and 23 are even more sustained. Both chapters go to great lengths to describe feminised Israel's adulteries (16:15–29, 30–34, 36; 23:5, 11–21) which are then followed up with accounts of violent punishments (16:27; 23:9–10, 22), which include public stripping (16:37, 39; 23:10, 26, 29), violent destruction, and mutilation (16:40–41; 23:25, 28–31, 46–47). As in Hosea there is in Ezekiel 16 a disconcerting shift from violence to calmness, even claims to affection (Ezek 16:42; Hos 2:14, Heb 2:16), and to reinstating the covenant (Ezek 16:60–63; Hos 2:18, Heb 2:20). This shift has sometimes been likened to the tactics of a domestic abuser (Setel 1985).[67]

Another association between marriage and violence pertains to intermarriage. Sometimes inter-ethnic marriage receives no pejorative comment; hence, Joseph receives Asenath daughter of Poti-phera, priest of On (namely, an Egyptian wife) from Pharaoh (Gen 41:45), and Moses receives Zipporah, daughter of the priest of Midian (Exod 2:16–21), as well as taking a Cushite wife (Num 12:1) – with not much further ado.[68] But on other occasions exogamy is vociferously condemned. Rebekah complains about her son Esau's Hittite wives (Gen 27:46), for example, and Isaac charges their other son, Jacob, to marry one of his maternal cousins (Gen 28:1–2). Very clear, too, is the account where Solomon is faulted for his foreign wives who led him astray. 1 Kings 11 describes how Solomon loved (from '*aha*b) many 'foreign women' (v.1), including 'from the nations of which the LORD had said to the Israelites, "None of you shall join them and none of them shall join you, lest they turn your heart away to follow their gods"' (v.2). But Solomon cleaved (from *d-b-q*) to such women for love (from '*aha*b) (v.2). It is not so much the large number of Solomon's wives, as their 'foreignness' and worship of 'foreign' gods that is condemned and blamed for luring Solomon into idolatry (1 Kgs 11:3–10, cf. Exod 34:15–16; Deut 7:2–4; and Neh 13:26). Of particular interest here is the unequivocal expression of divine objection to intermarriage; after all, God's direct speech is quoted (1 Kgs 11:2) to make this absolutely clear.

The Bible contains passages, which violently enforce divine objection to intermarriage. Let us cite a few key examples. First, in Numbers 25 is the account of events at Baal-peor where an Israelite man 'came and brought' a Midianite woman. The couple is later identified as Zimri, son of a chief, and Cozbi, daughter of a tribal head (Num 25:14–15). It is not unlikely that theirs was some kind of quasi-aristocratic wedding, or similar union, which the text depicts as an act of brazen abhorrence.[69] Horror is averted only by the fatal action of Phinehas the priest, who takes a spear and impales both the man and the woman 'through the belly' (Num 25:8). The implication is that the couple was having sex (consummating their marriage?) in their chamber when stabbed to death. This violent act by Phinehas is divinely approved (Num 25:13).

More clear condemnation of intermarriage comes in two books named after revered religious reformers: Ezra and Nehemiah. Ezra 9–10 and Nehemiah 13 impress on the community of descendants of the Exile who had returned to

Judah that all who had taken wives from the people of the land had to divorce them and send former wives and any children born from intermarriages away. Ezra depicts intermarriage as defiling the 'holy seed' (9:2), as an act of forsaking divine commandments (9:10), as unclean and an abomination (9:11),[70] as evil and a great sin (9:13). The condemnation is laid on thick. The way forward is a covenant (*berit*) with God to evict the women and children (10:3). Covenant here does not form but *dissolves* marriage.[71] The text continues that the wives and children are indeed sent away (10:44), which is surely an act of violence. It is likely to have been distressing (cf. Gen 21:11) – for the men, the women, and the children. The evicted are likely to have faced a precarious and frightening future exposing them to yet more violence.

The book of Nehemiah also places emphasis on 'God's law, which was given by Moses' (Neh 10:29, cf. 13:1–3). It is in accordance with this law that the promise is made not to intermarry with 'the peoples of the land' (Neh 10:30), because this is deemed evil and a betrayal of God (Neh 13:27). Judean men with foreign wives are cursed, beaten, have their hair pulled, and coerced into taking an oath (Neh 13:25). Again, violence is prominent.

Finally, another veritable 'elephant in the room' is that marriage in the Greek Bible is very prominently reflected on in decidedly negative terms. While Ephesians 5 is central to complementarian theology of marriage, other texts tend to receive rather less focus (Mackie 2023). Paul praises celibacy over marriage (1 Cor 7:7–8) and depicts marriage as a concession, a way of averting *porneia* ('sexual immorality', 1 Cor 7:2–4). As Mary Rose D'Angelo points out, 'Marriage is a form of bondage for both a man (1 Cor 7:27) and a woman (1 Cor 7:39). To be unmarried or released from marriage is analogous to emancipation from enslavement (1 Cor 7:21–24, 27, 39) (D'Angelo 2014: 498). This view of marriage is hardly edifying! In the gospels, too, Jesus sometimes demands that loyalty to him requires rejection of family, including one's spouse (Lk 14:26). Jesus concedes that not everyone is cut out for eschewing marriage (Mt 19:10–12). He is depicted as saying that marriage has no place in the resurrection (Mk 12:25; Mt 22:30). Instead, marriage is of 'this age' not of the worthier age to come (Lk 20:34–36), again with the effect of denigrating marriage.

In summary, marriage in the Bible is regularly signified by such actions as 'taking' and 'going in to', usually with no allusion to consent or mutuality. This is already suggestive of violence. But marriage is also often explicitly associated with violence – including with events we would today call war crimes, rape, enslavement, racism, intimate partner violence, and coercive control. We are not suggesting that constructions of biblical marriage advocate for such violations; but refusing to point out the presence of such horrors, while claiming that 'the Bible' offers a clear and consistent guide for 'biblical marriage' is disingenuous. Much of what 'the Bible' describes regarding relationships between men and women should not be dignified with the designation 'marriage' – and we firmly reject the violence of multiple kinds described and sometimes advocated and even sanctified in the biblical text.

Complementarian biblical marriage idealises one kind of union only – a sexually exclusive, committed 'covenant' before God, between one man and one woman, for life, with the man leading and the woman submitting. It argues that this kind of marriage *only* is 'natural' and proper and that it is clearly proclaimed in 'the Bible'. This is defended by using selective passages and applying these to scaffold a predetermined ideology. Other passages, which do not fit, are not mentioned, or not emphasised. The ideology condemns some things that receive only little, no, or at best ambiguous, mention in the Bible – such as homosexuality or gender fluidity. It does not condemn matters that appear unambiguously in at least some parts of the Bible – such as rape marriage and forced separation of inter-ethnic marriages. Spousal abuse, while it receives mention in the Bible, is not prominently condemned either. It does not, for instance, make it into Köstenberger's list of six sins that have corrupted biblical marriage.

We are not closed to the idea that there are successful and fulfilling complementarian marriages. But for very many the idealisation of biblical marriage is unhelpful. Indeed, both the growing literature from within Christian communities, testifying to spiritual abuse, including sexual and domestic forms of abuse, and the divorce rate among Christians, affirm the reality that the complementarian agenda is by no means always effective.

Indeed, just as Christian communities are not exclusively populated by consistently kind, selfless, heterosexual persons who can live up to the presumed high ideals of biblical marriage, so the texts of the Bible show evidence of a precarious and violent world. Hence, there are laws prohibiting adultery (Exod 20:14; Lev 20:10; Deut 5:18), coveting (Exod 20:17; Deut 5:21) and sex with family and household members (e.g., Lev 18:6–16), which surely would not exist unless persons felt and acted on temptation to commit such deeds. There are other mentions of violence speckled throughout the Bible – including violence leading up to or in marriage. Hence, Laban enjoins Jacob not to harm his wives (Gen 31:50), and there is mention of women being harassed when they work in the fields (Ruth 2:9), and raped when they go to visit other women (Gen 34:1–2), or dance with other women (Judg 21:21), in towns and in fields (Deut 22:23, 25; cf. Neh 5:5).

The presence of sexual predation evident in these passages is one point in common between the world reflected in biblical texts and the present (Stiebert 2020a). A second shared feature is that of evidence of change over time concerning marriage practices. Marriage is not static or timeless in 'the Bible' and it is not static in our context either. In the texts of the Bible there appears to be some shift from polygyny towards normalising monogamy,[72] and from levirate marriage (Gen 38:8; Deut 25:5–6) towards outlawing it (Lev 18:16; 20:21); intermarriage seems to be uncomplicated in some settings but not others, and consanguine (e.g., Gen 29:12) and even sometimes close-kin marriages (Gen 20:12) seem to have been acceptable, but not always (Lev 18:9; 20:17; cf. Mk 6:17–18). There is also fluidity in terms of household and family structures (Brenner 2010). Similarly, in our lifetime, there have been, in the UK, changes in terms of marriage law. Rape in marriage is now criminalised; same-sex civil unions and marriages are enshrined in law, as are same-sex parenting and adoption; most recently, the marriage age was raised to 18. A fixed and static picture of 'what marriage looks like' is represented neither in the Bible nor the world we are living in.

Before turning our attention to why any of this – that is, how marriage is depicted and linked with violence in the Bible, how this differs from what is promoted by biblical marriage – matters, we will briefly examine three of the proof-texts most widely cited in discussions on marriage and the Bible.

Genesis 1–3

The creation stories of Genesis 1–3 have been much and variously interpreted. They are pivotal in discussions of biblical marriage and, as already cited, one writer in RBMW asserts, 'as Genesis 1–3 go, so goes the whole Biblical debate … on manhood and womanhood' (Ortlund, in RBMW 2006: 95). But the same text is also read differently. Hence, for Deryn Guest, 'The creation stories do not so much reflect a divinely ordained sex/gender system as construct it' (Guest 2014: 288). Whereas RBMW sees the biblical text as containing a unifying thread, culminating in fulfilment in the Greek Bible and providing a blueprint for exclusive, complementary biblical marriage, Guest observes a very mixed collection of texts where gender norms are sometimes restricted and contained but at other times subverted and reconfigured. The divine creation of 'male and female' (Gen 1:27) is sometimes understood as signifying 'male and female *only*': that is, the creation of two complementary sexes to the exclusion of all others. The verse could also be interpreted as 'male and female *among others*' or as 'male, female and other categories in between, along a spectrum'.

Similarly disjunctive is interpretation of Genesis 2:24. Köstenberger claims that this verse, 'sets forth the biblical pattern as it was instituted by God at the beginning: one man is united to one woman *in matrimony*, and the two form one new natural family' (Köstenberger 2011: 2, italics added). But, awkwardly, matrimony receives no mention here (or anywhere in the three chapters, certainly not explicitly). Azzoni says of the same verse, 'Although many see Genesis 2:24 as presenting the ideal of marriage…, the passage does not mention the institution per se; … The verse… is presented as descriptive rather than prescriptive' (Azzoni 2014: 483). Hunter, too, is cautious, stating it is 'not an unreasonable interpretation' to read 2:24 as having 'some bearing at least by implication on the state of marriage' (Hunter 2011: 4). But he also says that 'it is again significant that no specific reference to marriage as an institution is indicated, nor can it be concluded that this bond is unique or indissoluble' (Hunter 2011: 4–5).

The reason for emphasis on these chapters in Christian contexts may well be that Jesus refers to Genesis 1:27 and 2:24 in a story from the gospel of

Mark (10:1–9). In this story 'Pharisees'[73] test Jesus by asking whether divorce, as described in Mosaic law, is permissible. Jesus goes back to the creation story, concluding, 'Therefore what God has joined together, let no one separate' (v.9). In a private teaching, Jesus adds that remarriage after divorce is adultery – both for a man and a woman (Mk 10:11–12). This could be read as an injunction to marry for life, with absolutely no option for divorce, because remarriage would risk committing one of the most reviled of all crimes, adultery. Indeed, this is how the passage *is* widely read. However, such unequivocal interpretation might be counterbalanced by two features. First, Jesus appears to prescribe other things that are difficult, even impossible to achieve – giving away all one has (Mk 10:21; cf. Mt 5:42), excising all conflict and feelings of lust (Mt 5:21–28), submitting to evildoers (Mt 5:38–40), and being perfect (Mt 5:48). It might, therefore, be the case that marriage for all time is, like these other inculcations, an ideal, possibly sometimes an unachievable one, and possibly not one that is to be pursued at any and all cost, or where failure to live up to the ideal is not unusual or unexpected. Jesus concedes that he demands that which is impossible for anyone other than God (Mk 10:27). Second, Jesus is also recorded as saying plenty that does not advocate for marriage and family life. His life is that of an itinerant, not a family man (Mt 8:20; Lk 9:58) and he expects the same of his followers (Lk 9:61–62). This is most clear when he says, 'Whoever comes to me and does not hate father and mother, wife and children, brothers and sisters, yes, and even life itself, cannot be my disciple' (Lk 14:26).

In the light of this portrayal of marriage in some of the stories of Jesus, Carolyn Mackie, who describes herself as growing up 'with evangelicalism's centring of marriage and family, supported by the mutually reinforcing ideologies of purity culture and marriage culture' (Mackie 2023), is justified in asking 'Why are so many Christians so focused on marriage?' (Mackie 2023). She goes on to draw attention to the story of the 'Sadducees'[74] who ask Jesus whether a woman who has consecutively married seven men would be resurrected with any which one or with all her husbands (Lk 20:27–40).[75] Mackie points out that this story receives considerably less attention in biblical marriage literature than Ephesians 5 but that 'Given that this is one of the only times that Jesus directly addresses marriage, it should be a seminal text for anyone trying to build a Christian understanding of marriage' (Mackie 2023). Jesus's pronouncement in response to the Sadducees' question is that marriage has no place in resurrected life. Not only might this, again, take away from the tremendous value and focus accorded to marriage in complementarian literature but it also signifies another renegotiation and revision of earlier laws and conventions. RBMW makes much of Jesus going back to Genesis 2:24 but this story in Luke (as well as in the other synoptic gospels) also nullifies the command to procreate (Gen 1:28). Instead, as Mackie discerns, 'Neither marriage nor procreation is a concern in the age to come' (Mackie 2023).[76]

Genesis 1–3, then, has been interpreted in diverse ways. Its relevance or otherwise to the topic of marriage requires projecting or inserting marriage into the text. Moreover, any reading of Genesis 1–3 is affected by how and alongside which other texts it is interpreted. A union of a man and a woman – let's call it marriage – and procreation may be interpreted as either significant, divinely enjoined, and permanent, or as passé, a thing rendered irrelevant alongside more important matters, such as the kingdom of God and resurrection.

Ephesians 5:21–33

This passage belongs to a group of Greek Bible texts called the Household Codes, which address ethical instructions concerning relationships of various kinds, notably those of husbands and wives, but also of parents and children, and enslavers and enslaved. Ephesians 5 is very widely cited in complementarian theology.

Complementarians in particular interpret the opening exhortation, for both partners in a couple to be subject to the other 'out of reverence for Christ' (v.21), as expressing a well-balanced, harmonious, reciprocity.[77] Added to this is that a husband is to love his wife like his own body and the identification of marital union (again referencing Genesis 2:24) as a great mystery (*mysterion*, Eph 5:32) and an imitation of Christ's self-sacrificial love for the church. Those who express reservation about this passage tend to point to the wife's subjection to her husband, who is her 'head' (5:22–23). 'Wives submit to your husbands' is an instruction, worded with some variations, also elsewhere (Col 3:18; 1 Pet 3:1; cf. 1 Cor 14:34–35[78]). Here wives' submission, or subjection, pertains to 'everything' (5:24).[79] Moreover, while a man should love his wife as himself, a wife should 'respect' (NRSV), or 'fear' (another legitimate meaning of *phobētai*) her husband (5:33).[80] While RBMW makes the case that husbands' headship and wives' submission is the marital ideal and fulfils the scheme created in Genesis 2, where the woman is created as 'helper' for the man, others reject the passage as enabling exploitation, even abuse. Paynter both acknowledges the way the text has been used abusively and defends its sacred value, while not agreeing uncritically with the notion of its enduring authority (Paynter 2020: 40). She concedes that sacred texts, including Ephesians 5, cannot be lifted from their specific context and projected, unmodified, on to the twenty-first century[81] and describes it as both 'revolutionary' in its own time, and 'not the final step' (Paynter 2020: 38–39).

Mackie challenges the very prominence that is accorded to marriage as a symbol for Christ's relationship with the church, from which are extrapolated the roles of each partner in a marriage. The effect of this, she argues, is to privilege this one metaphor, 'thereby granting marriage a special spiritual status' (Mackie 2023). And yet there are, she points out, a variety of other metaphors to express the relationship between Christ and the church: 'shepherd and flock, vine and branches, cornerstone and building' (Mackie 2023). And yet 'most people would not claim from this that raising sheep is a spiritually privileged occupation or that buildings are inherently sacramental'

(Mackie 2023). Indeed, as Mackie emphasises, Ephesians 5 itself draws also on another metaphor for Christ and the church: that of a body (5:29–31). She concludes, 'So yes, I can look to marriage and see a symbol of Christ and the church. But I can also look to my own body and see the same thing' (Mackie 2023).

Once more, one text is read in diverse ways, and not only the text's content but also whether it is accorded privileged emphasis, or, instead, considered either alongside other texts or with special focus on its situational context determines interpretation.

Malachi 2

Divorce is presented in highly undesirable terms, to be practised as a last resort if at all, in several Greek Bible passages (notably, 1 Cor 7:10–16). In the Hebrew Bible, however, as already mentioned, divorce seems an uncomplicated matter. One apparent exception is Malachi 2. The NRSV translates portions of 2:13–14, which are widely drawn into arguments for condemnation of divorce, as 'do not let anyone be faithless to the wife of his youth. For I hate divorce, says the LORD, the God of Israel'. This sounds unequivocal. The problem is that while the English translation seems clear and unambiguous, the Hebrew text does not.

Paynter illustrates that this 'notoriously difficult passage' is translated variously (Paynter 2020: 68–69). As Hunter explains, the oracle begins with a general complaint about Judah's unfaithfulness and profanation of the covenant. This leads on to the personification of Judah – a metaphor familiar from other prophetic texts (notably, Hosea and Ezekiel). Here, however, Judah is represented not as a bride or wife but (mostly) as husband. As in some other biblical texts, there is confusion with grammatical gender: RBMW may assert the 'unbending and unchanging grammatical and historical reality of the Biblical texts in Greek and Hebrew' (Piper and Grudem 2006: 84, cited above), and Köstenberger may revile 'gender confusion' as sin (Köstenberger 2011: 11), but when it comes to grammatical gender in the Hebrew Bible, there is plenty.[82] Here (feminine) Judah has been disloyal and (masculine) Judah has defiled God's sanctuary and married the daughter of a foreign deity. Strikingly, there is reference here to witnessing a marriage: while witnesses are customary nowadays in wedding ceremonies, this does not receive mention elsewhere in the Hebrew Bible. Novel, too, is the mention of the *chaverâ* ('companion') as partner in marriage (Hunter 2011: 19).

Hunter finds the final verse of the oracle particularly puzzling. That which is hated (translated 'divorce' in NRSV) is not transparent: 'it is by no means obvious that we should use such a legal term [as divorce] here. And the parallel with "covering one's garment with violence" (for which there are no equivalents anywhere in the Old Testament) only serves to render the whole impossible to interpret' (Hunter 2011: 20). Paynter tries to make some sense of this verse with recourse to an expression in the book of Ruth that also involves a garment. To give some context, the expression belongs to the threshing floor scene where Ruth is confronting Boaz, her deceased husband's kinsman, to do his duty and marry her. Ruth implores Boaz to 'spread [his] cloak over [her]' (Ruth 3:9), which for Paynter signifies the protection afforded by marriage. With this in mind, Paynter speculates that, 'Malachi is referring to the bringing of violence into the marital home' and, further, that it is this which constitutes 'a breach of the marriage covenant' (Paynter 2020: 71). Ultimately, however, this passage is a confusing muddle, and we are inclined to agree with Hunter 'that it would be ill-advised to construct on such a basis anything about the practical nature of marriage [or] divorce' (Hunter 2011: 20).

Apparent from all three examples is that the meaning of biblical texts, including texts drawn on to prescribe gender roles and wifely submission, and to proscribe divorce, is far from clear, unambiguous, or univocal. This is because 'the Bible' does not 'say' anything but is, instead, read and interpreted. And this interpretation 'does not happen in a neutral, objective bubble' (Guest 2014: 292). In the concluding chapter, we will turn to why this matters.

Notes

1 Like the Ten Commandments and their prohibition against coveting one's neighbour's *wife* (Exod 20:17; Deut 5:21), Jesus' words imply that he is addressing men and that men are presumed to lust after women (cf. Lk 14:26, which also mentions a wife but not a husband, again betraying androcentrism).
2 In all these examples from the Hebrew Bible, the reason for divorce lies with the (actual or metaphorical) woman. She is adulterous, faithless, or otherwise transgressive (Jer 3:8; Isa 50:1), or she is displeasing in some other, non-specific way (Deut 24:1–3).
3 The process of textual fixing is different in Jewish and Christian traditions. In Jewish tradition, the authoritative and now fixed text is the Masoretic Text, most often following the Leningrad Codex (dated by its colophon to 1008CE). This text is faithfully copied, inclusive of acknowledged errors. These written features are preserved as *ketib* ('as written') even though *qere'* ('as read') sometimes reinterprets, verbally corrects, or qualifies *ketib*. Even when a manuscript dated to around 50BCE (i.e., significantly more ancient than the Leningrad Codex) was discovered among the Dead Sea Scrolls (4QSam[a]), bringing to light a whole paragraph that served to make better sense of the text now in 1 Samuel 10, this paragraph was not inserted into the Tanakh, the Jewish canon. It is *not* found in JPS translations but *is* included in the NRSV (marked as an insertion in an annotation). With the Greek Bible, the process of textual criticism and fixing has proceeded differently, using not one copy text but a pastiche of the texts deemed most reliable. This is why the story of Jesus and the men caught out in hypocrisy (more widely known as Jesus and the woman caught in adultery) appears in the Greek Bible (most often at John 7:53-8:11) even though it is not present in the oldest manuscript versions. On the complexity of textual formation of Bibles (it is impossible to speak of just one Bible) we recommend Schmid and Schröter (2021).
4 We are not suggesting that this construction of Pharisees conforms to historical realities. 'The Pharisees' appear to fulfil a primarily literary and ideological function; they are a foil to Jesus who emerges as triumphant and progressive over against

them. The foolishness of the Persians with their immovable laws appears to be another literary trope, designed to showcase the wisdom and bravery of Judeans like Daniel, Esther, and Mordecai.
5 There is a documentary on BBC Sounds, 'Samburu: The fight against child marriage'.
6 One illustration of this is several sets of enslavement laws (Exod 21:2–11; Lev 25:39–55; Deut 15:12–18). These are not identical, indicating continuing acceptance of enslavement but also changes in recommended practice over time. With marriage law, there are also signs of change and misalignment. Hence, Deut 25:5–10 details what has come to be known as levirate marriage (named after Latin *lēvir*, 'husband's brother'), where a childless widow bears a child for her deceased husband through impregnation by her brother-in-law (cf. Gen 38:6–11). This practice cannot be reconciled with the so-called incest laws of Leviticus (Lev 18:16). A custom somewhat reminiscent of levirate marriage is also recorded in Ruth, where it is referred to as 'the custom in former times' (Ruth 4:7), again attesting to changes over time.
7 Historical investigations focused on religion and Bible usage make this very clear. Stone's social history of marriage and the family in England from 1500 to 1800 shows how the Bible came to the fore in the domestic realm from the early seventeenth century (Stone 1979: 104). Stone shows that in times when children were regarded as in need of control and suppression, texts such as Proverbs and Sirach came to the fore because these provided justification for harsh disciplining of children (Stone 1979:126). Similarly, as social attitudes changed towards favouring wifely submission, Stone explains, 'an ominous gloss to 1 Peter 3' appeared in Matthew's Bible of 1537 'that a husband, if his wife is "not obedient and helpful to him, endeavoureth to beat the fear of God into her head, and that thereby she may be compelled to learn her duty and do it"' (Stone 1979: 138). In other words, interpretation embellished 1 Peter 3 to legitimate physical disciplining of wives. The text of 1 Peter did not change but interpretation of it was sometimes expanded. Complementarianism, similarly, constructs a particular interpretation, fitting texts around an ideology.
8 See Holben (1999) for numerous examples along a spectrum extending from condemnation through to liberation.
9 In parts of the UK and elsewhere coverture laws, according to which upon marriage a woman's legal existence was merged into and entirely subordinated to her husband's, existed for centuries. The dissolution of such laws is not lamented, or even mentioned much, nowadays.
10 Wide acceptance of same-sex marriage in the UK, likewise, reflects societal attitudes and fuller understanding of human sexuality and orientation (cf. the Ozanne poll 2022).
11 Arguably, some cases of incest, where two closely related adults consent to sex and marriage even though the law of their country prohibits this, are more complicated. For much more on this, see Stiebert (2016: 1–18 and 2018a). These cases need not detain us here. Worth mentioning is that some countries and some religious codes permit marriages that UK law would deem illegal forced marriage, child marriage, and marriages deemed close-kin marriages in other jurisdictions but incestuous (meaning illegal) in UK law.
12 Hunter points out that the first creation story in Genesis 1, emphasising multiplying and dominion over all other life forms, is 'at odds with contemporary concerns about the environment'. He continues, 'Given the need to restrict human fecundity if the planet is to have a future, it might be necessary, therefore, to establish some distance between Cr[eation Story] 1 and our understanding of the marriage bond' (2011: 4). Hunter, therefore, is once more recommending a particular emphasis and selection for interpretation and application of biblical texts going forward. Again, this not only acknowledges but also advises dexterity in using biblical texts.

13 Most examples to follow come from the Hebrew Bible. As D'Angelo explains, 'attention to marriage and divorce is scattershot and limited' in the Greek Bible (D'Angelo 2014: 501).
14 The Christian site 'Got Questions?' in answering what a 'good Christian family' looks like according to the Bible, concedes that there *is no* biblical delineation of 'family' either – but then goes on, nonetheless, to claim what '[t]he biblical ideal of a family' is. See, https://www.gotquestions.org/Christian-family.html. The absence both of equivalent vocabulary and of systematic treatment of such concepts as 'marriage' or 'family' poses some difficulties in exploring the relevance of biblical texts for contemporary settings and situations regarding such topics. Like the advocates for 'biblical marriage', we will persist, following Hunter (2011), who argues for the possibility of forming some impression from biblical texts of family contexts and relationships.
15 The two words are contrasted in Hosea 2:16 (Heb 2:18).
16 One place where this is clear is in the Ten Commandments. These are addressed, it appears, to free male citizens. In the final commandment, the proscription applies to coveting one's neighbour's house, wife (or woman), male servant or female servant, ox or donkey, or anything else belonging to one's neighbour. Wife and servants are, therefore, bundled up with other possessions, such as livestock, suggesting that all, collectively, are a man's property (Exod 20:17; Heb 20:14). In the Catholic ordering of commandments, a distinction is made between sexual coveting (i.e., of the neighbour's wife) and coveting of possessions (i.e., of the neighbour's house and field, but also live 'property', namely servants, ox, and donkey, cf. Deut 5:21). Any distinction here is in degree rather than principle and androcentrism remains clear – not least, in the heteronormative address to a male and the absence of any reference to coveting one's neighbour's husband, or man. Notably androcentric, too, are the mentions in Proverbs to nagging, or quarrelsome wives (19:13; 21:9, 19; 25:24; 27:17) – never husbands. In the Greek Bible, meanwhile, it is unclear whether the man who has sex with his father's *gunē* is condemned for sex with his father's wife, or enslaved female (1 Cor 5:1–11). But the notion that women are property is clear (cf. also the reference to 'his virgin', 1 Cor 7:36–38).
17 A fine might be suggested in two legal texts (Exod 22:16–17; Deut 22:29). In the first example, a man who has had sex with an unbetrothed virgin must pay the *mohar* (bridewealth, or indirect dowry, see Lemos 2010: 38–39). Even if the woman's father refuses to 'give her (in marriage?)' to the man (rapist?), he still receives the *mohar* for virgins. This shows that a daughter, particularly a virgin daughter, is an economic commodity. For a very thorough discussion on *mohar* and on marriage gifts in the ancient world that provides context for the Bible see Lemos (2010).
18 The daughter of Pharaoh also receives a lavish gift: namely, a palace Solomon has built for her (1 Kgs 9:24). Rebekah, too, receives gifts on agreeing to marry Isaac (Gen 24:53).
19 Exod 21:7–8 indicates that a father could sell his daughter into enslavement, possibly into some form of marital and/or sexual, arrangement. On *'ahab*, see also notes 31 and 32.
20 The captive woman, brought to a man's house to be raped, cannot, should she displease the man for some unspecified reason, afterwards be sold (Deut 21:14). The verse acknowledges that the woman has been raped. The verb is a *piel* of the root *'-n-h*, which pertains to rape also elsewhere (Gen 34:2; Judg 19:24; 2 Sam 13:14).
21 As will be discussed, these passages are expressive of rape 'marriage'.
22 Hunter concedes that this kind of marriage 'may seem depressingly utilitarian' (Hunter 2011: 7). Yet even the story of Ruth, for all its idealisation as pastoral or pious idyll, or as romance (e.g., Grudem who sees 'foreshadowing of ... New Testament commands in the godly marriages... and honor given to women in passages

such as those in Ruth' (Grudem 2002: 36, n.23), is ultimately a story of a woman who marries a rich man and has his child to provide for her mother-in-law and herself. Liew's conclusion is particularly blunt: 'Naomi and Ruth work together so that a child is born to *Naomi* with the sperm of a displaceable or substitutable male candidate' (Liew 2009: 205).

23 Like Hagar, Bilhah, and Zilpah, too, are handed to their master to produce children (Gen 30:3–13). Enslaved women are taken and given to sons (Exod 21:7–9), or sons go ahead and just take them (Gen 35:22). With the exception, perhaps, of Reuben having sex with, possibly raping, 'his father's concubine' (Gen 35:22), which appears to have angered Jacob (cf. Gen 49:4), the other unions are recorded matter-of-factly enough and seem to signify some sort of marriage (i.e., legitimate, and accepted union). Hence, Bilhah, and Zilpah's sons have some degree of legitimacy and status (cf. Gen 49:16–21, 28). Children of secondary wives are not, however, guaranteed an inheritance (Gen 25:6).

24 Azzoni concurs, 'a man had sexual access to and agency over more than one woman in his household, whereas women were not legally allowed agency over their bodies. Women's sexuality was under the legal authority of their father (or occasionally brothers) before marriage and their husband after marriage' (Azzoni 2014: 483).

25 The verb refers at Judg 21:21, 23 to seizing or abducting women. If this is marriage, it is a form of marriage aptly called rape 'marriage'. Gafney (2009) interprets the verb's occurrence in the book of Ruth, where Naomi's sons 'lift up' Moabite women, Orpah and Ruth (as wives) (Ruth 1:4), as another instance of rape marriage.

26 'Taking' women one wants, sometimes on account of attraction, is modelled by the sons of God (Gen 6:2).

27 One more marriage verb discussed by Hunter is *chathan,* which occurs in the Hebrew reflexive *hithpael* form, 'which could arguably mean that the action implied has a reference both to its subject and its object… something like "to arrange a mutually beneficial alliance in marriage"' (Hunter 2011: 14). Hunter admits, however, that the verb overwhelmingly pertains to *inter*marriage (e.g., Shechem and Dinah in Gen 34 and Solomon and Pharaoh's daughter in 1 Kings 3, *pace* 1 Samuel 18, of David and Michal), which is likely to be more significant than reciprocity for the precise meaning.

28 Similarly, while 1 Cor 7 may be addressed to both men and women (e.g. v.16), the assumption is that any decision to marry rests with men (D'Angelo 2014: 498).

29 Hunter's research on marriage is available for download on the Shiloh Project site, https://www.shilohproject.blog/marriage-in-the-hebrew-bible/. We refer throughout to the longer of his two papers available there.

30 It is widely and, in our view, correctly, argued that Shechem rapes Dinah (e.g., Stiebert 2020: 25–26). Afterwards he 'spoke to the maiden's heart' (Gen 34:3). This could imply that Shechem is smitten with Dinah. The biblical text gives no insight into Dinah's perspective.

31 Hunter points out that this sole Hebrew word for 'love' 'is used of everything from the raw emotion that drives people into each other's arms to the most exalted divine relationship with humankind' (Hunter 2011: 2). The verb also refers to unexalted feelings, such as Amnon's infatuation or obsession with his sister Tamar (2 Sam 13:1), which transpires in rape (2 Sam 13:14).

32 Michal's unions with David and Palti show that she is entirely at the mercy of male agendas (see Thiede 2022b: 46–55). Thiede demonstrates that the narrator is 'less interested in Michal's love than in how her love can be leveraged' (Thiede 2022b: 47). There is one example of woman-to-woman love. Hence, the women of Bethlehem say of Ruth that she loves (from *'aha<u>b</u>*) Naomi, her mother-in-law (Ruth 4:15). For an intriguing and compelling Targum-inspired reading of the Ruth-Naomi-Boaz triad as a polyamorous relationship, see Kahn-Harris (2023). Also notable is Jonathan's reciprocated love for David (1 Sam 18:3; 20:17; 2 Sam 1:26).

33 The most widely used words for what might allude to marriage are 'taking' and 'giving (in marriage)' (*lqch* and *ntn*). Almost always these verbs take a male subject. Michal, too, is given to David by her father, Saul (1 Sam 18:21, 27), who later gives her to another man, Palti (1 Sam 25:44) (and maybe to an additional man, Adriel, as well, see the Hebrew text of 2 Sam 21:8). The exception is Sarai 'taking' her servant Hagar and 'giving' her to Abram her husband (*'ishah*) for a woman/wife (*'ishshâ*) (Gen 16:3). It is also men who 'know' (*yada'*, e.g., Gen 4:1, 17), or 'go in to' (*ba'*, 2 Sam 16:22), or 'lie with' (*sha<u>k</u>a<u>b</u>*, e.g., Gen 34:2) women, or who 'uncover (nakedness)' (*galah*, i.e., have deviant sex, e.g., Lev 18:14), again indicating an assumption of male sexual initiative.

34 See also Köstenberger: 'As the Song of Solomon makes clear, only in the secure context of an exclusive marital bond can free and complete giving of oneself in marriage take place' (Köstenberger 2011: 8). LLF discusses the Song in a section on 'Marriage and the Gift of Sex'. Others say 'the primary reference in its poetry of love is to sex as God's gift for the expression of the couple's love and the deepening of their life together' (Köstenberger and Jones 2020: 23). Not only is marriage projected on to this text, but also the assumption that the Song's poems praising a female body are by a male and those praising a male body by a female (envisaged as either the actual, imagined, or implied author), while maybe accurate, rests on heteronormative assumption. The headings assigning speakers, such as (male) 'lover' and (female) 'beloved' are not in the Hebrew text. Paynter (with focus on Eph 5) demonstrates the impact and possible distortion of imposing section headings (Paynter 2020: 27–28).

35 Hunter summarises and tabulates the 'striking range of language to do with the expression of love between a man and a woman' in the Song (Hunter 2011: 7, but see note 31 above), which includes not only *'aha<u>b</u>* but also multiple occurrences of *dod* ('love' or 'beloved').

36 Clines' argument that the Song, far from describing any actual encounters or relationship, is an erotic dream text ('a man's dream about a woman's love', Clines 1995: 103), one 'that verges on soft pornography' (1995: 101), 'written by an Israelite male to meet the desires and needs of other Israelite males' (Clines 1995: 99) is persuasive. Clines also concludes that the text is beguiling but with this – and because of this – 'a dangerous text' (Clines 1995: 121).

37 Hunter's examination does not discuss any possibilities of such practices edging into the territory of child exploitation, or child marriage. Instead, he draws attention to the positive remembrance of the partner of youth and suggests that young people could become friends, enjoying each other's company, and exploring together, before the onset of adult life, with adult restrictions and responsibilities.

38 Azzoni adds that Hagar here arranges the marriage for her son Ishmael, because they have been evicted from the family of Abraham. Consequently, she is by default the parent who arranges her son's marriage (Azzoni 2014: 485). In other words, this is not a passage that conveys mothers' equality in determining their children's futures but a situation of necessity.

39 There is also a description elsewhere of rejoicing in what may be a context of marrying (Isa 62:5; cf. Jer 7:34; 16:9; 25:10; 33:11). All the Jeremiah passages suggest that joyful sounds and expressions are associated with the groom and bride on the occasion of wedding.

40 The verb translated 'cleave' is from Hebrew *d-b-q*, which is also used of Ruth cleaving to Naomi (Ruth 1:14), preceding Ruth's words of loyalty (Ruth 1:16–17), which happen to appear regularly in same- and different-sex wedding ceremonies. On cleaving, see also p.34 note 45 above.

41 Grudem, in the first chapter of his edited volume, argues that the word translated 'desire' (*teshûqâ*) is a negative term, namely the woman's 'aggressive desire *against*

her husband' (Grudem 2002: 34). He argues against sexual desire, because, within marriage (as he argues applies here), such desire would be positive. Grudem continues, 'We should never try to promote or advocate Genesis 3:16 as something good!' (Grudem 2002: 35), meaning women should not strive against their husbands and men should not exert their physical strength in ruling over their wives. Unlike Trible, who argues that the hierarchical relationship whereby the man rules over the woman (3:16) comes from punishment and disrupts earlier egality ('once there was mutuality, now there is a hierarchy of division… the woman is corrupted in becoming a slave, and man is corrupted in becoming a master', 1978: 128), Grudem argues for pre-punishment 'perfect harmony, yet with a leadership role belonging to Adam as the head of his family' (Grudem 2002: 35).

42 The Hebrew term here is *'ednah*. BDB points out that the noun occurs only here and translates it 'delight (sexual)'.

43 The action is a participle from the root *ts-ch-q*, which also underlies the name Isaac. It is used, too, of what the Philistines want Samson to do (Judg 16:25), possibly to entertain them, dance for them, or be made sport of, or mocked. The action is translated 'playing' when applied to Ishmael's conduct (Gen 21:8, NRSV), an action that ignites Sarah to put pressure on Abraham to evict Hagar and Ishmael. Scholz proposes that the meaning of the root is sexually violent, as is most clear in the story of Potiphar's wife's invention of Joseph's sexual advances or harassment against her (Gen 39:14, 17). Scholz refers to Isaac's action that is observed by Abimelech as suggestive of rape (Scholz 2010: 91). Thiede identifies the scene as exploitative of Rebekah and as signifying voyeuristic collusion between Isaac and Abimelech (Thiede 2022a: 100–101). For an extended discussion of the verb, see Hunter (2011: 39–42).

44 Ng proposes that Elkanah's conduct towards Hannah potentially demonstrates coercive and controlling behaviour. Hence, Elkanah does not intervene in Peninnah's torment of Hannah and bombards Hannah with questions when she is weeping and unable to eat. Ng points out that Elkanah calls Hannah's heart 'bad' (not 'sad' as in the NRSV translation), possibly victim-blaming her. His flood of questions does not await answers and his enquiry as to why she is weeping and not eating might connote threat, or the accusation that she is being ungrateful in the face of his generosity. Also, Ng explains, Hannah does not have ten sons, so the only 'choice' Elkanah is giving her is loving him alone. Ng shows how all these align with patterns of coercive control (Ng 2023).

45 Though one should note the flipside, also in Proverbs, see note 16 above.

46 Robinson is right to note the undertone of loss, pain, and even violent severing, as the bride is told to 'forget' her people and her father's house (Ps 45:10–11) (Robinson 2022: 172).

47 This Hebrew verbal root pertains to marriage and technically refers to making (oneself) a daughter's husband. It could imply that exchanges of daughters forge unions between families, even whole communities. Such is indeed suggested by many passages in the Bible, albeit not always approvingly (e.g., Gen 34:9; Judg 21:1, 7).

48 Laban, Leah, and Rachel's father mentions a custom of not marrying a younger woman before her older sister (Gen 29:26). The marriage 'arrangement' is altogether blunt. Hence, Jacob approaches Laban after serving him seven years, saying 'Give me my woman/wife that I may go in to her' (Gen 29:21). This strikes us as a crass demand for penetrative sex.

49 Sometimes a man having sex with a woman appears to signify, or to confirm marriage (cf. Gen 29:21; and the rape in Deut 21:13). Such marriage seems to express above all that the man in the union has exclusive sexual access to the woman. David's illicit sex act with and rape of Bathsheba, however, occurs when Bathsheba is 'wife/woman of Uriah' (2 Sam 11:3–4). It is only after Uriah's death that David

sends for and brings her to his house to be 'his' woman/wife. The cruel machinations of Bathsheba's abuse are fully examined by Thiede (2022b: 55–65). Notably, Pharaoh, not knowing the nature of Abram and Sarai's relationship, 'took [Sarai] as [his] wife' (Gen 12:19).

50 In the Apocrypha, or deuterocanonical version, Tobit 7:13 mentions a marriage contract 'according to the decree of the law of Moses' but, as Hunter points out, what this decree might be is not clear (Hunter 2011: 16).

51 All four canonised gospels depict Jesus as bridegroom (Mt 9:15; Mk 2:19; Lk 5:35–36; Jn 3:29).

52 Prov 2:17, which rebukes the woman who forsakes the companion of her youth (her husband?) and (therewith?) disregards the covenant of her God (or gods) might chime well with Köstenberger but the covenant between David and Jonathan (1 Sam 18:1–3) would fail his 'sacredness' requirement that a covenant of marriage can exist only between a man and a woman (Köstenberger 2011: 6). Köstenberger seems unphased by the complete absence of divine criticism of polygamy (cf. Hunter 2011: 25) and, indeed, by laws casually mentioning or condoning both divorce (e.g. Exod 21:11; Lev 21:7, 14; 22:13; Num 30:9; Deut 22:29; 24:1–4) and polygyny (Exod 21:10; Deut 21:15–17; cf. Gen 25:6) that defy his criteria of permanence and exclusiveness.

53 We are unconvinced that 'the closest forms of human-to-human relationships' aptly capture how marital relationships are depicted in much of the Bible. While we have summarised some positive associations with marriage and weddings, there are also, as we go on to discuss, plenty of indications of violence in marriage. These are not confined to metaphors.

54 Sefaria translates *berit* 'pact' when it pertains to the bond between David and Jonathan, and 'covenant' in the Hosea passage. Multiple translations have 'covenant' (NRSV, NASB, KJV, ESV, NIV) but some have 'solemn pact' (NLT) or 'eternal friendship' (GNT).

55 As mentioned, this is not always between a man and woman pictured as a married couple. The covenant bond between David and Jonathan, and Ruth's loyalty to Naomi spring to mind. Added to this can be Ecclesiastes' touching image of two helping and keeping each other warm (Eccl 4:9–12). There is no obvious mention of marriage here.

56 Similarly, in the Greek Bible story of Jesus and the woman 'caught in the very act of committing adultery' (Jn 8:4) there is no naming or shaming of the co-responsible other person.

57 Other passages also express considerable control of husbands over wives (e.g., Numbers 30:6–16, with reference to a husband's divinely approved 'right' to validate or nullify his wife's vows).

58 There is plenty of evidence for this on the website and online publications of the multi-cultural Infidelity, Romantic Jealousy and Intimate Partner Violence Collaboration (https://www.lshtm.ac.uk/research/centres-projects-groups/jealousy-ipv-collaboration).

59 The two large volumes by CBMW edited by Grudem (2002) and Piper and Grudem (2006) barely mention Numbers 5 at all. The earlier volume makes no mention to the passage. The later volume refers to 5:18 to confirm that a woman's loosened hair might hint at suspicions of adultery and shame (Piper and Grudem 2006: 125, 126). This belongs to an argument concerning 1 Cor 11:2–16, which concludes, 'Paul calls on women to submit to their husbands' (Piper and Grudem 2006: 127).

60 Johanna discusses the full extent of this distressing law elsewhere (Stiebert 2019).

61 Johanna discusses this text more fully elsewhere (Stiebert 2022b).

62 As mentioned, the Hebrew word *'ishshâ* could also be translated 'woman', which would not explicitly convey the sense of a marriage. Indeed, here it may be better captured by a word such as 'breeder'.

63 If a man has sex with a married woman, or with a betrothed virgin in a populated setting, then both are to be killed (Deut 22:22–24). There is no opt-out for the eventuality that the woman is raped. The implication is that a virgin who is raped will cry out and be heard (Deut 22:24); but there are all kinds of easily imagined and plausible reasons why she might not cry out (notably, fear and the well-documented freeze response). Similarly, the death penalty is pronounced on both parties where a man 'lies with a male as with a woman' (Lev 20:13). Again, neither the age nor anything like consent is specified here. Hence, the prescription is that the death penalty also applies to a raped male child.
64 Johanna discusses this much more fully in a separate publication (Stiebert 2022b).
65 Translations render *'innitâh* in a variety of ways. NRSV has 'you have dishonoured her' and JPS has 'you had your will of her'. The *piel* of the verbal root *'nh* has a number of meanings. It refers clearly to situations of rape in other places where, as here, a male sexually abuses a female (Gen 34:2; 2 Sam 13:14). While the absence of a neat translation for the English designations 'marriage' or 'family' has not transpired in reluctance to apply them to the Bible, the word 'rape' has met with some hesitation and resistance. For a full and firm discussion on why it is important to call rape rape, see Thiede (2022: 3–11).
66 E.g., on Hosea, see Setel (1985); Weems (1995); and Sherwood (1996). On Ezekiel, see Galambush (1992); van Dijk-Hemmes (1995); Shields (1998); and Day (2000).
67 Violence of some kind in marriage is also acknowledged in the covenant between Laban and Jacob, where Laban seeks to secure that his daughters are not harmed (raped?) or supplanted by more wives (Gen 31:44–50) (and note 71).
68 Moses' siblings do express dissent concerning his Cushite wife (Num 12:1) and then challenge what they consider his exclusive claim to prophecy (Num 12:2). But Moses is vindicated by God himself (Num 12:4–9).
69 Sivan (2001) makes a compelling case for reading the story as a rape, where a family affair is instrumentalised to become a public and national spectacle.
70 The Hebrew word in this verse translated 'abomination' is *tô'ebâ* – the same word used for some kind of male-male sex-act in Lev 18:22 and 20:13. These verses of Leviticus are widely used to claim that 'the Bible' clearly condemns homosexuality. Inter-ethnic marriage, clearly maligned here and elsewhere in 'the Bible' in strong terms receives comparatively little attention in contemporary polemic (see Hunter 2011: 27). Again, this shows selective application of 'the Bible'.
71 Another use of 'covenant' (*berit*) ensures that Jacob not 'ill-treat' (NRSV, JPS) (or rape – again from the root *'nh*) his wives, the daughters of Laban (Gen 31:44–50).
72 D'Angelo points out that monogamy is, alongside passages of the Greek Bible, clearly enjoined in select Dead Sea Scrolls. Monogamy is required of the king, according to the Temple Scroll (11QT 56:17–19) and is inculcated in the Damascus Document (CD 4:20-5:1) (2014: 499).
73 See note 4. There is another version of the story in Matthew 19:3–9.
74 Like the 'Pharisees' (see note 4) the 'Sadducees' are a literary trope.
75 The story occurs also in both Matthew (22:23–33) and Mark (12:18–27).
76 Hunter is right to point out that 'while it is a commonplace of Christian teaching to understand the injunction to procreate as being exclusive to the institution of marriage, it is not obvious that this is the implication of Genesis 1' (Hunter 2011: 4).
77 For a similarly positive reading – moreover, in an edited volume focused on violence against women and children – interpreting submission as a call 'to meaningful bonding and accountability within a committed relationship', see Kroeger (1995: 140).
78 Husbands are enjoined to love their wives and never treat them harshly (Col 3:19), and to show consideration to their wives (1 Pet 3:7). 1 Peter also, however, concedes that not all husbands may do right. Nevertheless, wives are to attempt to win them over through their good conduct (3:1–2). In his discussion of 1 Peter, Carter

acknowledges '[t]he miasma of brutality and bullying that appears to float around this section' but will not go so far as to designate it 'a charter for domestic violence' (Carter 2020: 169). Carter's conclusion feels indecisive and, to us, uncomfortably reluctant to critically examine problematic aspects of the text.
79 Similarly, children (Col 3:20) and enslaved persons (Col 3:22) are instructed to obey 'in everything.'
80 For a full discussion on the verb 'to fear' in this passage, see Muers (Chaudhry, Muers, and Rashkover 2009: 196–197).
81 Paynter stresses that Paul's epistles are called 'occasional' documents for the very reason that they address 'specific purposes or occasions' (Paynter 2020: 35). This means that generalising from these documents may be particularly ill-advised. Richard Newton, similarly, likens the epistles of the Greek Bible to 'emails': i.e., both are texts written for an immediate purpose and with no intention or foresight that these would be canonised and scoured for meaning for centuries to come (Newton 2023).
82 See Guest (2011), on gender-switching in Judges, and Kahn-Harris (forthcoming) for examples from Ruth. For gender roles and ambiguity in the Bible, see Guest (2014) and Burke (2014).

3 Marriage, Bible, and Violence
Concluding Comments

The potential orbit of the various intersections between marriage, Bible, and violence is a very large one. It includes, for instance, that emphasis on procreation in biblical texts on marriage causes violence to those unable or unwilling to bear children; and it includes the violence of using the Bible to deny marriage to same-sex loving persons. In a small volume like this one, we cannot address the full spectrum of violence in contexts of marriage and Bible. We have centred our discussion above all on depictions of marriage in the Bible and on how 'marriage' bears violently on primarily Christian unions entered into willingly between a man and a woman.

In the preceding chapters, we have focused on how marriage is both discerned from and imposed on the Bible. Processes both of imposition and of biblical interpretation are ideologically charged in that they are not free of interests and agendas. Indeed, marriage is something of a magnet for ideological preoccupation. This is reflected in changes in marriage law over time, and accounts for its prominent presence in popular culture, including at the centre of polarising debates – in particular, the so-called 'culture wars' which often have the so-called 'homosexual agenda' and same-sex marriage at its heart.

The ideological claim that complementarian marriage is firmly inscribed in and prescribed by the Bible is powerful and far-reaching. We have focused primarily on examples from the USA where *both* a conservative Western Christian base *and* resources for production and dissemination are strongest. The circulation of complementarian texts by CBMW and FRC, among others, is considerable and extends well beyond the USA to many Christian communities across the world (see Shorter 2021; Koepping 2022). Its model for marriage claims to be grounded in all of tradition, nature, and God's word. It claims to distil what is allegedly clear in the Bible and further, that this model will protect against moral and social chaos and decay, envisaged as an absence of boundaries where sexual deviance and abuse are rampant. Central to complementarian agendas are that binary-gendered complementarian marriage is the godly original, present since creation (Gen 1–3), that a husband's headship and wife's submission are divinely ordained (Eph 5), and that divorce is ungodly (Mal 2). These are fitted into a wider network of ideologies

DOI: 10.4324/9781003152668-4

characterised by rejection of feminism, homosexuality, non-binaries of gender, and abortion, even if none of these receive much, or any, explicit mention in the Bible.

When we look at biblical passages on marriage *without* this scaffold of complementarian ideology, other facets emerge. Prominent among these is a strong association between marriage and violence – rape, coercive control, and battery. We acknowledge that choosing such an emphasis also reveals an ideological agenda. Indeed, we agree with Adryael Tong (2022) that *any* investigation of marriage and the Bible tends to take the form of looking to bolster pre-formed ideologies. As Tong makes clear, there is no 'unified voice' on marriage in the Bible, and claiming there is might say more about the interpreter than the text (Tong 2022).

One problem with complementarian biblical marriage is that it constructs and prescribes a marriage ideal where gentle women accommodate and submit to their strong, responsible husbands, where both are loving, respectful, selfless, as well as guided by a benign God and where this godly foundation resolves all obstacles. There is some admission that married life may get rocky and challenging, but divorce is not an option, except for 'in a very limited number of biblically prescribed circumstances' (Köstenberger 2011: 6).[1] While this is a rosy picture, it ignores, or at least downplays, the very many strains on relationships and marriages – such as financial strains, tensions and psychological stress on account of extended family, or childrearing, disagreements as to whether and when to have children, poor mental health, substance abuse, domestic violence and abuse, and infidelity, to name but a few.[2] The upshot of this is that rates of domestic abuse and divorce are not noticeably lower in Christian marriages in the USA or UK (places where data is available) than in the general population, just as sexual abuse, while far from exclusive to, is very much present in, religious, including church, communities.[3]

Rachel Starr writes that 'an idealized view of marriage, which fails to account for problems perpetuated by Christian teaching on marriage', such as 'prophetic descriptions of the covenant as a marriage, [that] does not acknowledge the violence of this metaphor and how it has been used to justify domestic violence over the centuries' has had profoundly damaging real-life consequence (Rachel Starr 2022). In challenging the church view of marriage, Starr asks, '[b]ut what if marriage was less of a gift and more of a problem?' She acknowledges that marriage *can* bring benefits, such as 'stability and friendship, as well as significant social and financial benefits' but also points to studies which show that married women have lower life expectancies and higher stress levels than single women, while married men have a higher life expectancy than single men. Starr suggests that maybe for women marriage is, conceivably, of negative, even life-limiting impact, something that publications such as LLF (and also those of CBMW and FRC) do not acknowledge (Rachel Starr 2022).

While our focus has been on Bible-using and above all Christian marriage settings, we have mentioned that abuse occurs in diverse religious settings also beyond Christian ones (Stiebert 2021). Joshua Brallier Shelton puts it aptly: abuse is 'a deeply human problem' and some forms, such as sexual and spousal abuse, are 'tied to hegemonic masculinity and the perverse manipulation of asymmetric power imbalances' (Shelton 2023).[4] Like many other feminists, we, too, argue that the gendered hierarchies promoted by complementarianism and supported by select biblical texts contribute to such abuse and violence, sometimes with devastating consequence. We consider neither religious authority figures nor sacred texts and interpretations innocent in this harm.

It is easy to speak of abusers as 'bad apples' and of applying sacred texts to justify or propel violence as 'misapplication' or 'misuse'. The *mis*use argument is not dissimilar to the 'guns don't kill people, *people* kill' argument. On the one hand, this may be true: after all, a gun locked up in a secure safe cannot kill; but a loaded gun in someone's hand, particularly in the hand of someone who is angry, and seeking to control and dominate and damage someone, is dangerous. On the other hand, rather obviously, gun crime and gun casualties always involve guns. To draw an analogy, scriptures, and religious authority (like guns) need not invariably cause or contribute to spiritual abuse; but when spiritual abuse occurs, they are often involved, especially when applied, or weaponised by someone controlling, domineering, or seeking to cause damage.

It is established beyond doubt that sexual abuse happens in religious communities, sometimes facilitated, and legitimated by, and sometimes silenced by, religious authority and scripture. It is also the case that domestic abuse (intimate partner violence, coercive control, and corporal punishment) happens in religious homes, sometimes using scripture to enable or justify such abuse. Scriptural and other religious authority is sometimes applied to circumvent secular law. Hence, religious leaders might not report abuse to police or legal authorities or might suppress information about sexual and domestic abuse in their communities. This is well attested,[5] and Saima has counselled victims of domestic violence who would not report their abuse because their abuser made them swear on their sacred text that they would not do so. Many persons active in religious communities have stories of shocking abuse to tell, including often attempts to repress their efforts of disclosure.

Our primary reason for stressing texts of marriage and violence has been to draw attention to *actual* violence in *actual* marriages, in particular Christian marriages where the Bible is most likely to have a presence and to be invoked. Idealisation and spiritualisation of marriage may conceal this, but violence in Christian marriages is real (Starr 2018: 41) – indeed, no less so than in the wider population. This is difficult to deny, given qualitative research in families (Westenberg 2017) and churches (Barnes and Aune 2021), as well as acknowledgement by church insiders (e.g., Radford and Cappel 2002; Hobbs 2020; Paynter 2020), including some testifying to personal experience at the hands of a church leader (Tucker 2016). Moreover, Valerie Hobbs argues not only that 'abuse rates in Christian homes ... [are] similar to societal rates' but also that '[r]eligious women are among the most vulnerable survivors of ... physical, sexual, or psychological harm by a current or former partner or spouse' (Hobbs 2020: 310). And this, we strongly believe, requires urgent calling out.

For all our focus on the Bible, we maintain that parallels can be drawn with other sacred texts and with those who use them in ways that inculcate gendered hierarchies. Indeed, some comparative investigations indicate this.[6] Sometimes, a case can be made for direct harm caused, where, for instance, a biblical text is weaponised to defend spousal abuse and spousal rape. Hence, Neil Elliott writes in *The Peoples' Bible* that '[p]rofessional social-work literature on women suffering domestic abuse showed that one of the anecdotally established indications that a woman was in imminent danger of suffering physical violence was that the man with whom she lived was quoting Paul's command that women be subject to their husbands' (Elliott 2009: 1633).

Beyond this direct and violent cause and effect, however, we insist also that silence causes violence. We see importance, therefore, in drawing attention to violence associated with marriage in the Bible that receives little attention and little calling out: precisely, because violence can flourish where there are denial, silencing, and suppression. Both idealisation of biblical marriage and silencing of those passages in the Bible which link marriage and violence can be reminders of the suppression of far-from-ideal and very real violence that takes place in marriages, including in Christian marriages. Lack of mention of topics such as intimate partner violence and domestic abuse and violence – be this in sermons, in prayers, or in readings or study of scripture, has, we argue, detrimental effects – such as silencing and diminishing the victims of such forms of abuse, and of collusion in the perpetuation of violence alongside its denial. Silence on abuse in marriage, particularly when this occurs alongside stressing male headship, or weaponising scriptures in other ways that determine power imbalances, we argue, proliferates violence and harm.

Among rarely mentioned biblical texts to which we have drawn attention are Numbers 5 and Numbers 31. Neither of these receives mention in the discussions on marriage of RBMW, Köstenberger, or LLF. We are not proposing they should determine guidance or law for marriage. After all, the former could all too easily be applied to condoning jealousy and coercive control (see Stiebert 2019), while the latter sanctifies rape 'marriage' of girl children (see Stiebert 2023). Yet Numbers 5 is one of the longest passages about a married couple and Numbers 31 is hauntingly reminiscent of the sexual abuse and exploitation of Yazidi women and girls of recent memory (Stiebert 2021). It might be said that Numbers 5 is odd, with its detailed ritual and magical potion bringing a curse – but is it odder than Genesis 1–3, very widely drawn on for discussion of biblical marriage (even though it never explicitly mentions marriage), with its talking serpent and magical fruit? And is not Numbers 5 disturbing alongside another passage widely drawn on in complementarian marriage, namely Ephesians 5? Ephesians 5 recommends male headship and female submission. Numbers 5, if read alongside this, condones male jealousy and suspicion, whether substantiated or not, and female submission to a frightening public ordeal. By not mentioning and not calling out such passages, we might collude in the suggestion that the Bible has clear, positive, and unambiguous directives on marriage. It silences abusive texts and abusive theologies that can be derived from them (Stiebert 2023).

Being silent about such texts also silences criticism of them. By extension, this can silence criticism of persons and interpretations deemed (like biblical texts) to be authoritative. And this is dangerous. As has become all too clear, religious figures in the highest ranks of authority (including popes and archbishops) have been plausibly accused of suppressing deplorable crimes. Religious leaders have been accused and convicted of terrible crimes – including sexual abuse and domestic battery. We would like to slightly adapt and to echo Stephen Young that 'the erasure of … violence and the silencing of victims have been crucial factors in keeping society hospitable to misogyny and rape' (Young 2022: 251), including with regard to domestic and spousal abuse. Young illustrates that in the book of Revelation the Son of Man is described as committing gendered violence. Given the authority of the canonised text and of the Son of Man, he points out, this 'becomes more than an abstract issue' (Young 2022: 251). It is worth here to quote Young at length:

> When it is normal to overlook sexual violence against women while reading the Bible, it will 'come naturally' for folks shaped by such reading cultures to overlook sexual violence in the world of their daily lives. Conversely, it will feel uncomfortable when they encounter people trying to make sexual violence that looks bad for patriarchy visible. … [I]nstitutions where upholding the Bible's 'moral reputation' is a paramount value will do so by overlooking its sextual violence, downplaying it, or blaming its victims…. This will especially be the case in settings where claims about the Bible's perfection or inerrancy authorize its authority. … It is a culture of identifying with exploitative misogyny, and… this culture has a long history of predictable consequences that are devastating to women, children, and also men who do not conform to gender norms. … If rape culture thrives on erasing, excusing, or downplaying sexual violence and silencing victims… [we need t]o reverse the scenarios…
> (Young 2022: 251).

Young's suggestion is that instead of suppressing the Son of Man's rape of Jezebel (Rev 2:20–23), we 'instead label this as gendered sexual violence committed by Jesus, but then unequivocally reject it' (Young 2022: 251). We are suggesting something comparable: namely, a much more candid and critical examination of biblical texts.

We are not saying that 'the Bible says (in Revelation) that the Son of Man is a rapist' or that God according to Hosea 1–3 is a wife beater. We are urging careful, critical reading of the biblical text that stays attuned to possibilities of textual toxicity. It is *uncritical* reading of metaphors such as those of Revelation and Hosea that can lead to normalising of and inattention to what they transmit. And such normalisation and lack of criticism can inure us also to uncritical or toxic interpretation of biblical texts.[7] Moreover, when it is acceptable and encouraged to critique and even reject what some biblical texts (e.g., Numbers 5 and 31, for instance) seem to promote, it can also create possibilities and permission to challenge not only texts and interpretations given authority but also persons with authority. Again, we argue, this is extremely important, because not only are there violent and abusive marriages that harm one or more persons in or affected by them, and, situations where biblical texts are used to augment violence, there are also abusers, including in positions of spiritual authority. This has been made abundantly clear in the very numerous sexual abuse scandals involving multiple Christian denominations and religious communities. Christa Brown (2009), Ruth Tucker (2016), Ruth Everhart (2020), and Miryam Clough (2022), are just four of very many more who all testify to abuse from religious leaders and to ineffectual church structures and processes failing victims, and not even believing or validating victims' claims. This speaks to profound and widespread systemic problems and shows that there is urgent need for enabling and encouraging critical thinking about authority wherever (in texts and interpretations) or by whomever it is claimed.

Saima's extensive experience over decades with those harmed by religious authorities and texts shows up very many and very real scars – psychological, emotional, spiritual, and physical. Saima describes cases where husbands, by analogy with religious metaphor, cast themselves as God and demand submission and reverence from wives. Any discord in the marriage and divorce, too, is widely blamed on wives.[8] Moreover, Saima reports how wives, in particular any aspersions about their conduct and sexual proclivities (real or imagined), are also held responsible for any stain on the reputation of the wider family.[9]

Saima has seen how legal protection or 'common sense' may have little sway over against the compelling power of religion and culture. Hence, domestic violence may be outlawed and divorce may be legally available, but religious authority can silence or overrule this on account of its stronghold over victims of spiritual abuse.

Yes, the Bible has inspired and motivated a wide range of individuals and actions, ranging from the sublime to the horrific. There is no indication that the Bible, or any other sacred text, is the root cause of violence, including violence in marriage. But it has also not prevented violence in religious settings and in marriage, or intimate partner violence, alongside other forms of family violence, such as corporal punishment of children. The previous two chapters have shown that biblical marriage is idealised. Yet, for all its claims to the importance of the Bible, the importance of careful study of its words, and to assertions of the Bible's power to cure societal ills, biblical marriage bases itself on selective choices of texts and sanitises out the many passages where violence in marriage is either implied or explicitly present. As already mentioned, marriage in communities, where the Bible is invoked as canonical, is *not* free from coercive control and domestic abuse. Indeed, these scourges seem not even to be significantly less prevalent there. Some claim that the problem lies not with the Bible but in its misapplication. Helen Paynter defends the Bible and its enduring support for the righteous and oppressed (Paynter 2020)[10] and Saima, too, sees harm as lying not with religion but with how religion is manipulated by those with power and status. Whether we acknowledge some degree of harm as deriving from the authority conferred on texts that link violence and marriage (Chapter 2), or locate harm in ideologies manipulating proof-texts (Chapter 1), there are crimes perpetrated against actual victims, human psyches, spirits, and bodies.

To conclude, this book has navigated two concurrent realities. First, biblical texts, like other sacred texts, remain influential and a focus of ongoing interpretation and scrutiny, most directly in communities of faith; and second, violence, including various forms of spiritual abuse, including within marriage, exists widely in the Bible's orbit of influence. Where this violence is repressed and silenced it also has detrimental effect. We have sought to work together, combining our perspectives, to ensure that our academic enquiry remains mindful of the survivors in our midst. We have tried to remember and to hear survivors of trauma who encounter biblical texts of violence, or interpretations of such texts. We have tried to demonstrate that activism – in this case, calling to account texts and interpretations of power – can be combined with research and that research can and should be directed towards activism.

In this we are far from singular and we have referred to other scholar-activists whose work is survivor-centred in a range of ways – in that it incorporates survivor voices (Blyth 2010; Klopper 2021), or fieldwork and co-reading (Tan 2021; van Klinken et al 2021), or autoethnography (van Klinken 2019; Clough 2022), for instance. We hope that this project in co-production will motivate more dialogue and more dialogic research and more activism against violence – right up until we won't need it any more.

Notes

1 The two exceptions are in cases of 'sexual immorality, that is, sexual marital unfaithfulness' (Mt 19:9) and if an unbelieving spouse wishes to divorce following their partner's conversion to Christianity (1 Cor 7:15) (Köstenberger 2011: 19). But even in cases of adultery, Köstenberger adds, 'divorce is only permissible, not encouraged or even preferable' (Köstenberger 2011: 19). Notably, no allowance is made for escape from relatively commonplace and acutely damaging situations such as coercive control or domestic violence. For the most part, Köstenberger characterises divorce as a symptom of 'independent-minded, freedom-worshipping, individuality rights-exalting culture' (Köstenberger 2011: 5) – in other words, as flighty and selfish.
2 On reasons for divorce and an overall picture that dispels the idea of divorce on a selfish or frivolous whim, see Scott et al (2013).

3 Over recent decades, sexual abuse scandals have been exposed in very many and diverse communities and settings, including the police, armed forces, schools, universities, sports clubs, hospitals, and foster homes. Abuse in religious contexts, or spiritual abuse, is not exclusive to churches and Christianity (Stiebert 2021). There have, however, been multiple scandals in many countries and Christian denominations. This reveals among other things that publicly condemning sexual abuse or showing that passages of the Bible condemn sexual abuse, does not prevent sexual abuse, or ensure that when it does happen it is dealt with promptly and effectively.

4 Shelton (2023) addresses both general patterns within religious abuse and the need for culturally specific nuancing.

5 Both of us have on multiple occasions encountered frustration from police, social services, and legal representatives who report that religious leaders often attempt to deal with matters deemed 'difficult' or 'private' in-house, rather than seeking professional help or reporting crimes. Reports by IICSA (the Independent Inquiry into Child Sexual Abuse) also disclose how obstructive church bodies have been in terms of safeguarding and reporting abuse.

6 E.g., see the contributions on sexual violence and sacred texts of Judaism, Christianity, and Islam in Kalmanofsky (2017), as well as the comparative reading exercise on women and marriage by Chaudhry, Muers, and Rashkover (2009), and the research conducted on religious leader responses to domestic violence and abuse by Levitt and Ware (2006).

7 Blyth demonstrates how the metaphor of Hosea 1–3, associating the prophet Hosea's marriage to his unfaithful wife Gomer with God's covenant relationship with Israel, is presented in teen girl bibles to promote the forbearance and pain of Hosea and God while completely downplaying and, indeed, justifying the physical punishments inflicted on Gomer, who is stripped of clothes, deprived of water, starved of food, and held captive (Hos 2:1–13). As Blyth points out, the biblical text and its interpretation in 'Mirror Images' 'minimize and justify IPV by blaming the victims and heroizing the perpetrators' with the effect that '[t]eenage girls are effectively being told that women "deserve" violent abuse and control, and that they should "thank" and "praise" a God who mandates deadly gender violence'. She concludes, rightly, 'It's unconscionable' (Blyth 2021: 55). Tan, meanwhile, describes reading Hosea 1–3 with sex workers in Hong Kong. Tan recounts how distressing the text is to them, with the public stripping perceived as 'gratuitous and malicious… humiliating and traumatising' (Tan 2021: 75).

8 This finds ready recognition in marriage metaphor analogies of God and disobedient Israel (Hos 1–3) and Christ and church (Eph 5).

9 Attitudes of honour and shame and double standards concerning women's sexual conduct vis-à-vis men's are, again, easily recognised in the Bible (see our discussion of Numbers 5 and Warren 2022).

10 E.g., 'But the Bible does not support the abuse of anyone. It can only appear to do so if it is manipulated and twisted' (Paynter 2020: 18). Saima concurs with this, whereas Johanna finds some biblical texts hard to exonerate.

Works Cited

'Abortion'. The Council on Biblical Manhood and Womanhood. Available online: https://cbmw.org/resources/?category=27#posts (accessed 21 July 2021).

Alves, Maria Juscinaide Henrique, Jeanderson Soares Parente, and Grayce Alencar Albuquerque. May–August 2016. 'Homosexual Orientation in Childhood and Adolescence: Experiences of Concealment Ad Prejudice'. *Reprodução & Climatério* 31/2: 68–75. Available online: https://doi.org/10.1016/j.recli.2016.03.002.

Avisa Project. Available online: https://avisa.huma-num.fr/s/avisa-english/page/home (accessed 18 October 2021).

Ayers, David J. 2006. 'The Inevitability of Failure: The Assumptions and Implementations of Modern Feminism'. In RBMW, pp.312–331.

Azzoni, Annalisa. 2014. 'Marriage and Divorce: Hebrew Bible', pp.483–488, in Julia M. O'Brien (ed. in chief), *The Oxford Encyclopedia of the Bible and Gender Studies*. Oxford and New York, NY: Oxford University Press.

Bailey, Wilma Ann. 2005. *'You Shall Not Kill' or 'You Shall Not Murder'? The Assault on a Biblical Text*. Wilmington, DE: Michael Glazier.

Barnes, Rebecca and Kristin Aune. 2021. 'Gender and Domestic Abuse Victimisation among Churchgoers in North West England: Breaking the Church's Gendered Silence'. *Journal of Gender-Based Violence* 5/2: 271–288.

Barr, Beth Allison. 2021. *The Making of Biblical Womanhood: How the Subjugation of Women Became Gospel Truth*. Grand Rapids, MI: Brazos Press.

BBC Sounds. 6 September 2022. 'Samburu: The Fight against Child Marriage'. The Documentary Podcast. Available online: https://www.bbc.co.uk/programmes/p0cyl404 (accessed 26 April 2023).

Berlin, Adele and Marc Zvi Brettler (eds.). 2004. *The Jewish Study Bible* (Jewish Publication Society). Oxford and New York, NY: Oxford University Press.

Blyth, Caroline. 2010. *The Narrative of Rape in Genesis 34: Interpreting Dinah's Silence*. Oxford: Oxford University Press.

Blyth, Caroline. 2021. *Rape Culture, Purity Culture, and Coercive Control in Teen Girl Bibles*. London and New York, NY: Routledge.

Blyth, Caroline, Emily Colgan, and Katie B. Edwards (eds.). 2018. *Rape Culture, Gender Violence, and Religion: Biblical Perspectives* (Religion and Radicalism). Cham, Switzerland: Palgrave Macmillan.

Blyth, Caroline, Emily Colgan, and Katie B. Edwards (eds.). 2018. *Rape Culture, Gender Violence, and Religion: Christian Perspectives* (Religion and Radicalism). Cham, Switzerland: Palgrave Macmillan.

Works Cited

Blyth, Caroline, Emily Colgan, and Katie B. Edwards (eds.). 2018. *Rape Culture, Gender Violence, and Religion: Interdisciplinary Perspectives* (Religion and Radicalism). Cham, Switzerland: Palgrave Macmillan.

Blyth, Caroline and Prior McRae. 2018. '"Death by a Thousand Paper Cuts": Transphobia, Symbolic Violence, and Conservative Christian Discourse', pp.111–133, in Caroline Blyth, Emily Colgan, and Katie B. Edwards (eds.), *Rape Culture, Gender Violence, and Religion: Interdisciplinary Perspectives* (Religion and Radicalism). Cham, Switzerland: Palgrave Macmillan.

Boyarin, Daniel. 2004. *Border Lines: The Partition of Judaeo-Christianity* (Divinations: Rereading Late Ancient Religion). Philadelphia, PA: University of Pennsylvania Press.

Brenner, Athalya. 2010. 'Alternative Families: From the Hebrew Bible to Early Judaisms'. *Journal of Early Christian History* 21/2: 39–50.

Brettler, Marc Zvi. 2005. *How to Read the Bible*. Philadelphia, PA: JPS.

Brown, Christa. 2009. *This Little Light: Beyond a Baptist Preacher Predator and His Gang*. Cedarburg, WI: Foremost Press.

Brown, Donald E. 1991. *Human Universals*. New York, NY: McGraw Hill. (Kindle Version).

Buchanan, Patrick ('Pat'). 1992. 'Culture War' Speech. Address to the Republican National Convention. Houston, Texas. Available online (Voices of Democracy: The U.S. Oratory Project): https://voicesofdemocracy.umd.edu/buchanan-culture-war-speech-speech-text/ (accessed 11 December 2021).

Burke, Sean D. 2014. 'Gender Transgression: New Testament', pp.304–310, in Julia M. O'Brien (ed. in chief), *The Oxford Encyclopedia of the Bible and Gender Studies*. Oxford: Oxford University Press.

Byrd, Aimee. 2020. *Recovering from Biblical Manhood & Womanhood: How the Church Needs to Rediscover Her Purpose*. Grand Rapids, MI: Zondervan Reflective.

Carden, Michael. 2006. 'Genesis/Bereshit', pp.23–60, in Deryn Guest, Robert E. Goss, Mona West, and Thomas Bohache (eds), *The Queer Bible Commentary*. London: SCM.

Carter, Steve. 2020. 'A Charter for Domestic Violence? The Subordination of Slaves and Wives in 1 Peter', pp.168–190, in Helen Paynter and Michael Spalione (eds.), *The Bible on Violence: A Thick Description* (Bible in the Modern World, 73; Sheffield Institute for Interdisciplinary Biblical Studies Monographs, 1). Sheffield: Sheffield Phoenix.

Chaudhry, Ayesha S. 2017. 'Naming Violence: Qur'anic Interpretation between Social Justice and Cultural Relativism', pp.95–124, in Amy Kalmanofsky (ed.), *Sexual Violence and Sacred Texts* (Feminist Studies in Religion). Indianapolis, IN: Dog Ear Publishing.

Chaudhry, Ayesha S., Rachel Muers, and Randi Rashkover. 2009. 'Women Reading Texts on Marriage'. *Feminist Theology* 17/2: 191–209.

Clines, David J. A. 1995. *Interested Parties: The Ideology of Writers and Readers of the Hebrew Bible*. (JSOTSup 205; Gender, Culture, Theory 1). Sheffield: Sheffield Academic Press.

Clines, David J. A. 2020. 'The Ubiquitous Language of Violence in the Hebrew Bible', pp.23–41, in Jacques van Ruiten and Koert van Bekkum (eds.), *Violence in the Hebrew Bible* (Oudtestamentische Studiën/Old Testament Studies 79). Leiden: Brill. Available online: https://www.academia.edu/37260426/The_Ubiquitous_Language_of_Violence_in_the_Hebrew_Bible (accessed 6 November 2022).

Works Cited

Clough, Miryam. 2022. *Vocation and Violence: The Church and #MeToo*. London and New York, NY: Routledge.

Cobb, Christy and Eric Vanden Eykel (eds.). 2022. *Sex, Violence, and Early Christian Texts*. London: Lexington Books.

D'Angelo, Mary Rose. 2014. 'Marriage and Divorce: New Testament', pp.497–502, in Julia M. O'Brien (ed. in chief), *The Oxford Encyclopedia of the Bible and Gender Studies*. Oxford and New York, NY: Oxford University Press.

Day, Linda. 2000. 'Rhetoric and Domestic Violence in Ezekiel 16'. *Biblical Interpretation* 8: 205–230.

Dobash, R. Emerson and Russell Dobash. 1979. *Violence against Wives*. New York, NY: Free Press.

Domoney-Lyttle, Zanne. 18 September 2018. 'The Handmaid's Jail: Framing Sexual Assault and Rape Narratives in Biblical Comics'. The Shiloh Project. Available online: https://www.shilohproject.blog/the-handmaids-jail-framing-sexual-assault-and-rape-narratives-in-biblical-comics/ (accessed 25 March 2023).

Du Mez, Kristin Kobes. 2020. *Jesus and John Wayne: How White Evangelicals Corrupted a Faith and Fractured a Nation*. New York, NY: Liveright.

Ebeling, Jennie R. 2010. *Women's Lives in Biblical Times*. London and New York, NY: T&T Clark.

Edwards, Katie B. 2015. *Rethinking Biblical Literacy*. London and Oxford: Bloomsbury.

Eisner, Will. 2006. *The Plot – The Secret Story of the Protocols of the Elders of Zion*. New York, NY: W. W. Norton and Co.

Elliot, Elisabeth. 2006. 'The Essence of Femininity: A Personal Perspective'. In RBMW, pp.394–399.

Elliott, Neil. 2009. *The Peoples' Bible: NRSV with the Apocrypha*. Minneapolis, MN: Fortress Press.

Everhart, Ruth. 2020. *The #MeToo Reckoning: Facing the Church's Complicity in Sexual Abuse and Misconduct*. Downers Grove, IL: InterVarsity Press.

Fea, John, Laura Gifford, R. Marie Griffiths, and Lerone A. Martin. November 2018. 'Evangelicalism and Politics'. *The American Historian*. Available online: https://www.oah.org/tah/issues/2018/november/evangelicalism-and-politics/ (accessed 22 October 2020).

Ferguson, Sian. No date. 'Cisgender and Straight Don't Mean the Same Thing – Here's Why.' Available online: https://www.healthline.com/health/cisgender-vs-straight#learn-more (accessed 14 August 2021).

Gafney, Wilda. 2009. 'Mother Knows Best: Messianic Surrogacy and Sexploitation in Ruth', pp.23–36, in Cheryl A. Kirk-Duggan and Tina Pippin (eds.), *Mother Goose, Mother Jones, Mommie Dearest: Biblical Mothers and Their Children*. Atlanta, GA: Society of Biblical Literature.

Galambush, Julie. 1992. *Jerusalem in the Book of Ezekiel: The City as Yahweh's Wife* (Society of Biblical Literature Dissertation Series, 130). Atlanta, GA: Scholars Press.

Gevisser, Mark. 2020. *The Pink Line: The World's Queer Frontiers*. London: Profile Books.

Glahn, Sandra. 24 June 2014. 'Was Abigail Right to Go Behind Nabal's Back?' Available online: https://blogs.bible.org/was-abigail-right-to-go-behind-nabals-back/ (accessed 13 September 2021).

Got Questions. Your Questions. Biblical Answers. 'How Does the Bible Define a Good Christian Family?' Available online: https://www.gotquestions.org/Christian-family.html (accessed 13 February 2023).

Works Cited

Greenough, Chris. 2021. *The Bible and Sexual Violence against Men*. Abingdon, OX and New York, NY: Routledge.

Gretton-Dann, Judith. 8 January 2021. 'Is It a Duty to Be Beautiful?' The Shiloh Project. Available online: https://www.shilohproject.blog/is-it-a-duty-to-be-beautiful/ (accessed 19 November 2021).

Grudem, Wayne (ed.). 2002. *Biblical Foundations for Manhood and Womanhood*. Wheaton, IL: Crossway.

Grudem, Wayne. 2016. 'If You Don't Like Either Candidate, Then Vote for Trump's Policies'. Available online: https://www.waynegrudem.com/wp-content/uploads/2016/10/If-You-Dont-Like-Either-Candidate-Then-Vote-for-Trumps-Policies.pdf (accessed 19 February 2021).

Guest, Deryn. 2011. 'From Gender Reversal to Genderfuck: Reading Jael through a Lesbian Lens', pp.9–43, in Teresa J. Hornsby and Ken Stone (eds.), *Bible Trouble: Queer Reading at the Boundaries of Biblical Scholarship*. Atlanta, GA: SBL.

Guest, Deryn. 2014. 'Gender Transgression: Hebrew Bible', pp.287–293, in Julia M. O'Brien (ed. in chief), *The Oxford Encyclopedia of the Bible and Gender Studies*. Oxford: Oxford University Press.

Guest, Deryn, Robert E. Goss, Mona West, and Thomas Bohache. 2006. *The Queer Bible Commentary*. London: SCM Press.

Gur, Haviv Rettig. 31 May 2020. 'How Ultra-orthodox Parties Became the Biggest Winners in Israel's New Government'. *The Times of Israel*. Available online: https://www.timesofisrael.com/how-the-ultra-orthodox-parties-became-biggest-winners-in-israels-new-government/ (accessed 22 October 2020).

Haaken, Janice, Holly Fussell, and Eric Mankowski. 2007. 'Bringing the Church to Its Knees: Evangelical Christianity, Feminism, and Domestic Violence Discourse'. *Psychotherapy and Politics International* 5: 103–115.

Harris, Christopher E. July 2003. '50 Years Ago in The Journal of Pediatrics: Homosexual Behavior in Children'. *The Journal of Pediatrics* 143/1: 80. Available online: https://doi.org/10.1016/S0022-3476(03)00253-1.

Hobbs, Valerie. 2020. 'Rape Culture in Sermons on Divorce', pp.309–328, in Helen Paynter and Michael Spalione (eds.), *The Bible on Violence: A Thick Description* (Bible in the Modern World, 73; Sheffield Institute for Interdisciplinary Biblical Studies Monographs, 1). Sheffield: Sheffield Phoenix.

Holben, L. R. 1999. *What Christians Think about Homosexuality: Six Representative Viewpoints*. BIBAL Press.

Hunter, Alastair G. 2011 (posted 24 May 2021). 'Marriage in the Old Testament'. Available online for download: https://www.shilohproject.blog/marriage-in-the-hebrew-bible/.

IICSA (Independent Inquiry into Child Sexual Abuse). Available online: https://www.iicsa.org.uk (accessed 7 May 2023).

Infidelity, Romantic Jealousy and Intimate Partner Violence Collaboration. London School of Hygiene & Tropical Medicine. Available online: https://www.lshtm.ac.uk/research/centres-projects-groups/jealousy-ipv-collaboration (accessed 22 March 2023).

International Academy for Marital Spirituality (INTAMS). Available online: http://www.intams.org (accessed 18 February 2021).

Johnson, Andy J. (ed.). 2015. *Religion and Men's Violence against Women*. New York, NY: Springer.

Johnson, Michael P. 2005. 'Domestic Violence: It's Not about Gender — Or Is It?'. *Journal of Marriage and Family* 67: 1126–1130.

Kahn-Harris, Deborah. 2023. *Polyamory and Reading the Book of Ruth*. Pennsylvania, PA: Lexington Press.

Kalmanofsky, Amy (ed.). 2017. *Sexual Violence and Sacred Texts* (Feminist Studies in Religion). Indianapolis, IN: Dog Ear Publishing.

Kaziimba, Most Rev. Dr. Stephen Samuel. 10 February 2023. 'Letter; Church of Uganda Responds to Church of England's Decision to Bless Same-Sex Unions'. Available online: https://boonafm.com/letter-church-of-uganda-responds-to-church-of-englands-decision-to-bless-same-sex-unions/ (accessed 27 March 2023).

Klopper, Frances. 2021. '"On, That I Had Wings Like a Dove…" Psalm 55 and Breaking the Silence about Violence against Women'. *Old Testament Essays* 34/1: 285–299.

Knight, George W. III. 2006. 'How Should Biblical Manhood and Womanhood Work Out in Practice?' In RBMW, pp.345–357.

Koepping, Elizabeth. 2022. *Spousal Violence among World Christians: Silent Scandal*. London: Bloomsbury Academic (paperback edition).

Köstenberger, Andreas J. 2011. 'The Bible's Teaching on Marriage and Family'. Family Research Council. Available online: https://downloads.frc.org/EF/EF11J34.pdf (accessed 19 November 2020).

Köstenberger, Andreas J. with David W. Jones. 2010. *God, Marriage, and Family* (2nd edn.). Wheaton, IL: Crossway.

Kroeger, Catherine Clark. 1995. 'Let's Look again at the Biblical Concept of Submission', pp.135–140, in Carol J. Adams and Marie M. Fortune (eds.), *Violence against Women and Children: A Christian Theological Sourcebook*. New York, NY: Continuum.

Langenberg, Amy and Ann Gleig. 1 October 2020. 'From *Sudinna* to the *Sangha Sutra*: Classical and Contemporary Buddhist Responses to Sexual Misconduct.' A Presentation for the Centre for Religion and Public Life Seminar, University of Leeds. Available online: https://religioninpublic.com/2020/10/26/crpl-seminar-series-from-sudinna-to-the-sangha-sutra-classical-and-contemporary-buddhist-responses-to-sexual-misconduct-oct-2020/ (accessed 2 November 2020).

Lemos, T. M. 2010. *Marriage Gifts and Social Change in Ancient Palestine – 1200 BCE to 200 CE*. Cambridge and New York, NY: Cambridge University Press.

Levitt, Heidi M., and K. N. Ware. 2006. 'Religious Leaders' Perspectives on Marriage, Divorce, and Intimate Partner Violence'. *Psychology of Women Quarterly* 30/2: 212–222.

Liew, Tat-siong Benny. 2009. 'Learning to Know about Others Who "Know Best"', pp.201–210, in Cheryl A. Kirk-Duggan and Tina Pippin (eds.), *Mother Goose, Mother Jones, Mommie Dearest: Biblical Mothers & Their Children*. Atlanta, GA: SBL.

Living in Love & Faith: Christian Teaching and Learning about Identity, Sexuality, Relationships and Marriage. 2020. London: Church House Publishing.

Lynch, Gordon. 2021. *UK Child Migration to Australia 1945–1970: A Study in Policy Failure* (Palgrave Studies in the History of Childhood). Cham: Palgrave Macmillan. Available for free download: https://link.springer.com/book/10.1007%2F978-3-030-69728-0

Mackie, Carolyn. 20 March 2023. 'Dearly Beloved, We Are Children of the Resurrection'. Women in Theology. Available online: https://womenintheology.org/2023/03/20/dearly-beloved-we-are-children-of-the-resurrection/ (accessed 14 April 2023).

Matthews, Shelly and E. Leigh Gibson (eds.). 2005. *Violence in the New Testament*. New York, NY and London: T&T Clark.

Morse, Holly. 2020. *Encountering Eve's Afterlives: A New Reception Critical Approach to Genesis 2–4* (Oxford Theology & Religion Monographs). New York, NY: Oxford University Press.

Moscowitz, Leigh. 2013. *The Battle over Marriage: Gay Rights Activism through the Media*. Urbana, Chicago, and Springfield, IL: University of Illinois Press.

Murdock, George P. 1945. 'The Common Denominator of Cultures', pp.123–142, in Ralph Linton (ed.), *The Science of Man in the World Crisis*. New York, NY: Columbia.

Newton, Richard. 28 February 2023. 'Why the US Gun Epidemic Is Also a Scriptural Pandemic'. The Shiloh Podcast (Episode 13). Available on Spotify.

Ng, Yannis. 2023. 'Comfort or Cajole: Reading Elkanah's Response to Hannah with the Awareness of Coercive Control'. *A Paper Presented at the Society for the Study of Theology Conference* (Warwick University, UK, 19 April 2023). Available online: https://www.shilohproject.blog/comfort-or-cajole-reading-elkanahs-response-to-hannah-with-the-awareness-of-coercive-control/ (accessed 24 April 2023).

ONS (Office for National Statistics). 14 April 2020. 'Marriages in England and Wales: 2017'. Available online: https://www.ons.gov.uk/peoplepopulationandcommunity/birthsdeathsandmarriages/marriagecohabitationandcivilpartnerships/bulletins/marriagesinenglandandwalesprovisional/2017 (accessed 23 October 2020).

O'Rourke Boyle, Marjorie. 2001. 'The Law of the Heart: The Death of a Fool (1 Samuel 25)'. *Journal of Biblical Literature* 120/3: 401–427.

Ortlund, Eric. 14 February 2023. 'The Song of Songs for Singles'. Available online: https://www.desiringgod.org/articles/the-song-of-songs-for-singles (accessed 15 February 2023).

Ortlund, Raymond C., Jr. 2006. 'Male–Female Equality and Male Headship: Genesis 1–3'. In RBMW, pp.95–112.

Ozanne Foundation. 2022. 'Same Sex Marriage Research 2022'. Available online: https://ozanne.foundation/project/same-sex-marriage-research-2022/ (accessed 17 January 2023).

Parnass, Sarah. 4 April 2013. 'Republicans Predict Fraud, Bestiality if Gay Marriage Is Legalized'. *ABC News*. Available online: https://abcnews.go.com/blogs/politics/2013/04/republicans-predict-fraud-bestiality-if-gay-marriage-is-legalized (accessed 24 January 2023).

Patterson, Dorothy. 2006. 'The High Calling of Wife and Mother in Biblical Perspective'. In RBMW, pp.364–377.

Paynter, Helen. 2020. *The Bible Doesn't Tell Me So: Why You Don't Have to Submit to Domestic Abuse and Coercive Control*. Abingdon, OX: The Bible Reading Fellowship.

Perriello, Pat. 26 August 2013. 'Trouble with Celibacy in the Church in Africa'. National Catholic Reporter. Available online: https://www.ncronline.org/blogs/ncr-today/trouble-celibacy-church-africa (accessed 14 August 2021).

Pew. 2014. https://www.pewforum.org/religious-landscape-study/marital-status/divorcedseparated/

Phillips, Peter M. 2020. *The Bible, Social Media and Digital Culture*. Abingdon, OX and New York, NY: Routledge.

Piper, John. 2006. 'A Vision of Biblical Complementarity: Manhood and Womanhood Defined According to the Bible.' In RBMW, pp.31–59.

Piper, John. 2006. 'Foreword: For Single Men and Women (and the Rest of Us).' In RBMW, pp.xvii–xxviii.

Works Cited

Piper, John and Wayne Grudem (eds.). 2006 [1991]. *Recovering Biblical Manhood & Womanhood: A Response to Evangelical Feminism*. Crossway. Available online: https://document.desiringgod.org/recovering-biblical-manhood-and-womanhood-en.pdf?ts=1471470614 (accessed 12 February 2021).

Piper, John and Wayne Grudem. 2006. 'An Overview of Central Concerns: Questions and Answers'. In RBMW, pp.60–92.

Poythress, Vern Sheridan. 2006. 'The Church as Family: Why Male Leadership in the Family Requires Male Leadership in the Church'. In RBMW, pp.345–357.

Radford, Lorraine and Cecilia Cappel. 2002. 'Domestic Violence and the Methodist Church – the Way Forward: The Report and Recommendations on Domestic Violence and the Methodist Church'. Methodist Conference 2002 Report. Available online: https://www.methodist.org.uk/downloads/conf-domestic-violence-the-way-forward-2002.pdf (accessed 22 April 2023).

Reaves, Jayme R. 2020. 'Reading the Whole Bible with Integrity: Identifying Context, Identity, Community, and Antisemitism in Christian Hermeneutical Practices'. *Journal for Interdisciplinary Biblical Studies* 2/1: 150–178.

Reinhartz, Adele. (Winter–Spring) 2000. 'Margins, Methods, and Metaphors: Reflections on a Feminist Companion to the Hebrew Bible'. *Prooftexts* 20/1–2 (Reading Through the Lens of Gender): 43–60.

Reissig, Courtney. 2015. *The Accidental Feminist: Restoring Our Delight in God's Good Design*. Wheaton, IL: Crossways.

Robinson, Laura. 2022 'Ambivalent Wedding Imagery in Matthew's Jerusalem Narrative', pp.169–183, in Christy Cobb and Eric Vanden Eykel (eds.), *Sex, Violence, and Early Christian Texts*. Lanham, MD: Lexington Books.

Rollens, Sarah, Eric Vanden Eykel, and Meredith J. C. Warren. 2020 'Confronting Judeophobia in the Classroom'. *Journal for Interdisciplinary Biblical Studies* 2/1: 81–106.

Sáenz-Badillo, Angel.1993. *A History of the Hebrew Language*. Transl. by John Elwolde, Cambridge: CUP.

Schäfer-Bossert, Stefanie. 1994. 'Den Männern die Macht und der Frau die Trauer? Ein kritischer Blick auf die Deutung von *'ôn* – oder: Wie nennt Rahel ihren Sohn?', pp.102–123, in Hedwig-Jahnow Projekt (ed.), *Feministische Hermeneutik und Erstes Testament: Analysen und Interpretationen*. Stuttgart: Kohlhammer.

Schmid, Konrad and Jens Schröter. 2021. *The Making of the Bible: From the First Fragments to Sacred Scripture*. Cambridge, MA and London: Belknap Press.

Scholz, Susanne. 2010. *Sacred Witness: Rape in the Hebrew Bible*. Minneapolis, MN: Fortress Press.

Schreiner, Thomas R. 2006. 'Head Coverings, Prophecies, and the Trinity: 1 Corinthians 11:2-16'. In RBMW, pp.124–139.

Scott, Shelby B., Galena K. Rhoades, Scott M. Stanley, Elizabeth S. Allen, and Howard J. Markman. 2013. 'Reasons for Divorce and Recollections of Premarital Intervention: Implications for Improving Relationship Education'. *Couple, Family, Psychology* 2/2: 131–145. DOI: 10.1037/a0032025. Available online: https://www.ncbi.nlm.nih.gov/pmc/articles/PMC4012696/ (accessed 21 March 2023).

Setel, T. Drorah. 1985. 'Prophets and Pornography: Female Sexual Imagery in Hosea', pp.86–95, in Letty M. Russell (ed.), *Feminist Interpretation of the Bible*. Oxford: Basil Blackwell.

Shelton, Joshua Brallier. 17 April 2023. 'Opinion: We Need to Think about the Dalai Lama's Actions Very Carefully'. Tricycle. Available online: https://tricycle.org/article/dalai-lama-actions/?fbclid=IwAR11s-aSE4xTnpQrKzUQA1y-HjS88KG1Fh4qYqT77l3vJrjLk4iNCwpr1474 (accessed 18 April 2023).

Sherwood, Yvonne. 1996. *The Prostitute and the Prophet: Hosea's Marriage in Literary-Theoretical Perspective* (Journal for the Study of the Old Testament Supplement, 212; Gender, Culture, Theory, 2). Sheffield: Sheffield Academic Press.

Shields, Mary E. 1998. 'Multiple Exposures: Body Rhetoric and Gender Characterization in Ezekiel 16'. *Journal for Feminist Studies in Religion* 14: 5–18.

Shorter, Rosie Clare. 2021. 'Rethinking Complementarianism: Sydney Anglicans, Orthodoxy and Gendered Inequality'. *Religion and Gender* 11: 218–244.

Sivan, Helena Zlotnick. 2001. 'The Rape of Cozbi (Numbers XXV)'. *Vetus Testamentum* 51/1: 69–80.

Sjoberg, Laura. 2016. *Women as Wartime Rapists: Beyond Sensation and Stereotyping*. New York, NY: New York University Press.

Stahl, Ashley. 1 May 2020. *New Study: Millennial Women Are Delaying Having Children Due to Their Careers*. Forbes (Careers). Available online: https://www.forbes.com/sites/ashleystahl/2020/05/01/new-study-millennial-women-are-delaying-having-children-due-to-their-careers/?sh=94b0249276ad (accessed 19 November 2021).

Starr, Rachel. 2018. *Reimagining Theologies of Marriage in Contexts of Domestic Violence: When Salvation Is Survival*. Abingdon, OX and New York, NY: Routledge.

Starr, Rachel. 8 September 2022. *What Is Marriage? Living in Love and Faith... And Denial*. ViaMedia News. Available online: https://viamedia.news/2022/09/08/living-in-love-and-faith-and-denial/ (accessed 8 September 2022).

Stiebert, Johanna. 2016. *First-Degree Incest and the Hebrew Bible* (LHBOTS 596). London and Oxford: Bloomsbury.

Stiebert, Johanna. 2018a. 'Brother, Sister, Rape: The Hebrew Bible and Popular Culture', pp.31–50, in Caroline Blyth, Emily Colgan, and Katie B. Edwards (eds.), *Rape Culture, Gender Violence, & Religion: Biblical Perspectives*. Cham, Switzerland: Palgrave Macmillan.

Stiebert, Johanna. 15 May 2018b. 'Interview with Saima Afzal: Founder of SAS RIGHTS'. The Shiloh Project. Available online: https://www.shilohproject.blog/interview-with-saima-afzal-founder-of-sas-rights/ (accessed 14 August 2021).

Stiebert, Johanna. 2019. 'Divinely Sanctioned Violence against Women: Biblical Marriage and the Example of the *Sotah* of Numbers 5'. *The Bible and Critical Theory* 15/2: 84–108.

Stiebert, Johanna. 2020. *Rape Myths, the Bible, and #MeToo*. Abingdon, Oxon and New York, NY: Routledge.

Stiebert, Johanna. 2021. 'Religion and Sexual Violence', pp.339–350, in Caroline Starkey and Emma Tomalin (eds.), *The Routledge Handbook of Religion, Gender and Society*. London: Routledge. DOI: 10.4324/9780429466953-25.

Stiebert, Johanna. 31 May 2022a. 'Abortion and the Bible'. The Shiloh Project. Available online: https://www.shilohproject.blog/abortion-and-the-bible/ (accessed 14 April 2023).

Stiebert, Johanna. 2022b. 'The Pop of Cherries and Weasels: Virgins, Violence and the Bible', pp.32–49, in Helen Paynter and Michael Spalione (eds.), *Global Perspectives on Bible and Violence* (Bible in the Modern World, 81; Sheffield Centre for Interdisciplinary Biblical Studies Monographs, 5). Sheffield: Sheffield Phoenix.

Stiebert, Johanna. 2023. 'Abusive Theology and LLF'. *Modern Believing* 64/1: 8–16.

Stiebert, Johanna. 2024 (Forthcoming). 'Abigail', in Lena-Sofia Tiemeyer and David Shepherd (eds.), *The Oxford Handbook of King David*. Oxford and New York, NY: Oxford University Press.

Stone, Ken. 2015. 'Marriage and Sexual Relations in the World of the Hebrew Bible', pp.173–188, in Adrian Thatcher (ed.), *The Oxford Handbook of Theology, Sexuality, and Gender*. Oxford: OUP.

Stone, Lawrence. 1979. *The Family, Sex and Marriage in England 1500-1800*. Harmondsworth, Middlesex: Penguin.

Taduggoronno, Lavinia. 17 August 2022. 'Lambeth Conference 2022: The History, The Division and the Way Forward'. Anglican Ink. Available online: https://anglican.ink/2022/08/17/lambeth-conference-2022-the-history-the-division-and-the-way-forward/ (accessed 25 April 2023).

Tan, Nancy Nam Hoon. 2018. 'Response: Between Resisting White and Reflecting Black: A Hong Kong Resident's Response and Perspective', pp.57–75, in Johanna Stiebert, and Musa W. Dube (eds.), *The Bible, Centres and Margins: Dialogues between Postcolonial African and British Biblical Scholars*. London: Bloomsbury T&T Clark.

Tan, Nancy Nam Hoon. 2021. *Resisting Rape Culture: The Hebrew Bible and Hong Kong Sex Workers*. Abingdon, OX and New York, NY: Routledge.

Thatcher, Adrian. (8 Dec.) 2020. *Living in Love and Faith*. Modern Church: Faith in the World. Available online: https://modernchurch.org.uk/adrian-thatcher-living-in-love-and-faith (accessed 29 October 2022).

Thatcher, Adrian. 2021. 'Living in Love and Faith'. *Marriage, Families & Spirituality* 27/1: 36–48. DOI: 10.2143/INT.27.1.3289473.

The Shiloh Project: Rape Culture, Religion and the Bible. Available online: https://www.shilohproject.blog (accessed 23 October 2020).

Thiede, Barbara. 2022a. *Male Friendship, Homosociality, and Women in the Hebrew Bible: Malignant Fraternities*. Abingdon, Oxon, and New York, NY: Routledge.

Thiede, Barbara. 2022b. *Rape Culture in the House of David: A Company of Men*. Abingdon, Oxon, and New York, NY: Routledge.

Thiede, Barbara. 2023. 'Disruption, Disorder, and Death: Eve (and Lilith) in Classical Rabbinic Literature', pp.74–87, in Caroline Blyth and Emily Colgan (eds.), *The Routledge Handbook on Eve*. New York, NY: Routledge.

Tomalin, Emma. 2023. 'Spiritual Abuse and Gender Based Violence', pp.323–334, in Parveen Ali and Michaela Rogers (eds.), *Gender-Based Violence: A Comprehensive Guide. For Nurses and Healthcare Providers*. New York, NY: Springer.

Tombs, David. 2023. *The Crucifixion of Jesus: Torture, Sexual Abuse, and the Scandal of the Cross*. Abingdon, Oxon, and New York, NY: Routledge. Available open access: https://www.taylorfrancis.com/books/oa-mono/10.4324/9780429289750/crucifixion-jesus-david-tombs?context=ubx&refId=df17dbb8-76f1-46f3-8b89-8460a5cd7246.

Tong, M. Adryael. 2022. 'Jesus, Marriage, and Sexuality', *Theology and Religion Online*. Bloomsbury Publishing DOI: 10.5040/9781350893221.007. Available online: https://www.theologyandreligiononline.com/article?docid=b-9781350893221&tocid=b-9781350893221-007&st=tong

Trible, Phyllis. 1978. *God and the Rhetoric of Sexuality*. Philadelphia, PA: Fortress Press.

Tucker, Ruth A. 2016. *Black and White Bible, Black and Blue Wife: My Story of Finding Hope after Domestic Abuse*. Grand Rapids, MI: Zondervan.

van Dijk-Hemmes, Fokkelien. 1995. 'The Metaphorization of Woman in Prophetic Speech: An Analysis of Ezekiel 23', pp.244–255, in Athalya Brenner (ed.), *A Feminist Companion to the Latter Prophets* (The Feminist Companion to the Bible, 8). Sheffield: Sheffield Academic Press.

van Klinken, Adriaan. 2019. *Kenyan, Christian, Queer: Religion, LGBT Activism, and Arts of Resistance in Africa*. University Park, PA: Penn State University Press.

van Klinken, Adriaan and Johanna Stiebert, with Sebyala Brian and Fredrick Hudson. 2021. *Sacred Queer Stories: Ugandan LGBTQ+ Refugee Lives and the Bible* (Religion in Transforming Africa Series). Woodbridge, Suffolk, and Rochester, NY: James Currey.

Warren, Meredith J. C. 2022. 'Five Husbands: Slut-Shaming the Samaritan Woman', pp.217–238, in Christy Cobb and Eric Vanden Eykel (eds.), *Sex, Violence, and Early Christian Texts*. London: Lexington Books.

Weems, Renita J. 1995. *Battered Love: Marriage, Sex, and Violence in the Hebrew Prophets* (Overtures to Biblical Theology). Minneapolis, MN: Augsburg Fortress.

Welby, Justin and John Sentamu (Signed as Justin Cantuar and Sentamu Eboracensis, on behalf of the House of Bishops of the Church of England). 2017. 'House of Bishops Pastoral Guidance on Same Sex Marriage'. Available online: https://www.churchofengland.org/sites/default/files/2017-11/House%20of%20Bishops%20Pastoral%20Guidance%20on%20Same%20Sex%20Marriage.pdf (accessed 29 August 2021).

West, Gerald O. 2019. 'Forging Tools, Framing Theory, for Faithful African Interpretations: A Response to Judith McKinlay'. *Bible & Critical Theory* 15/1: 23–28.

Westenberg, Leonie. 2017. '"When She Calls for Help"—Domestic Violence in Christian Families'. *Social Sciences* 6/3: 71, pp.1–10 (pdf version). DOI: 10.3390/socsci6030071. Available online: https://www.mdpi.com/2076-0760/6/3/71 (accessed 22 April 2023).

WHO. World Health Organisation. 'Violence'. Available online: https://www.who.int/groups/violence-prevention-alliance/ (accessed 26 April 2023).

Young, Stephen. 2022. 'Revelation Naturalizes Sexual Violence and Readers Erase It: Unveiling the Son of God's Rape of Jezebel', pp.239–259, in Christy Cobb and Eric Vanden Eykel (eds.), *Sex, Violence, and Early Christian Texts*. London: Lexington Books.

Index of Biblical References (following NRSV ordering)

Hebrew Bible

Genesis 1–3 19, 41, 46, 53–55, 58n12, 66, 69
Genesis 1 19, 30n17, 53, 54, 64n76
Genesis 2–3 19, 43
Genesis 2 9n14, 17, 31n27, 34n45, 43, 53, 54, 55
Genesis 3 19, 20, 43, 62n41
Genesis 4 20, 61n33
Genesis 5 30n17
Genesis 6 60n26
Genesis 12 63n49
Genesis 16 47, 61n33
Genesis 18 43
Genesis 19 19
Genesis 20 52
Genesis 21 43, 51, 61n38, 62n43
Genesis 24 43, 59n18
Genesis 25 60n23, 63n52
Genesis 26 43, 62n43
Genesis 27 43, 50
Genesis 28 50
Genesis 29 40, 43, 52, 62n48–49
Genesis 30 60n23
Genesis 31 52, 64n67, 64n71
Genesis 34 40, 42, 47, 52, 59n20, 60n27, 60n30, 61n33, 62n47, 64n65
Genesis 35 10n22, 60n23
Genesis 38 43, 45, 52, 58n6
Genesis 39 62n43
Genesis 41 50
Genesis 49 10n22, 60n23
Exodus 2 50
Exodus 15 21, 33n43
Exodus 20 38, 52, 57n1, 59n16
Exodus 21 32n33, 36, 40, 58n6, 59n19, 60n23, 63n52
Exodus 22 59n17
Exodus 34 50
Leviticus 18 19, 52, 58n6, 61n33, 64n70
Leviticus 19 18, 40
Leviticus 20 18, 19, 52, 64n63, 64n70
Leviticus 21 63n52
Leviticus 22 63n52
Leviticus 25 58n6
Numbers 5 28, 46–47, 49, 63n59, 69, 70, 71, 73n9
Numbers 12 33n43, 50, 64n68
Numbers 25 50
Numbers 30 63n52, 63n57
Numbers 31 27, 28, 40, 48–49, 69, 71
Numbers 36 40
Deuteronomy 4 36
Deuteronomy 5 52, 57n1, 59n16
Deuteronomy 7 50
Deuteronomy 15 58n6
Deuteronomy 21 27, 28, 40, 49, 59n20, 62n49, 63n52
Deuteronomy 22 18, 19, 21, 28, 47, 52, 59n17, 63n52, 64n63
Deuteronomy 23 24
Deuteronomy 24 37, 57n2, 63n52
Deuteronomy 25 52, 58n6
Deuteronomy 34 33n43
Joshua 1 22
Judges 1 47
Judges 4 6, 21
Judges 5 10n22, 21
Judges 6 22
Judges 11 28
Judges 14 42, 43, 47–48
Judges 15 47
Judges 16 62n43
Judges 19 19, 59n20
Judges 21 27, 49, 52, 60n25, 62n47
Ruth 1 60n25, 61n40

Index of Biblical References (following NRSV ordering)

Ruth 2 52
Ruth 3 57
Ruth 4 58n6, 60n32
1 Samuel 1 43
1 Samuel 10 57n3
1 Samuel 18 40, 42, 45, 47, 60n27, 60n32, 61n33, 63n52
1 Samuel 20 60n32
1 Samuel 25 17, 32n29, 43, 61n33
2 Samuel 1 60n32
2 Samuel 11 43, 62n49
2 Samuel 13 47, 59n20, 60n31, 64n65
2 Samuel 16 61n33
2 Samuel 21 61n33
1 Kings 3 43, 60n27
1 Kings 9 40, 59n18
1 Kings 11 50
2 Kings 5 22
2 Kings 22 21
Ezra 9–10 50
Ezra 9 51
Ezra 10 51
Nehemiah 5 52
Nehemiah 10 51
Nehemiah 13 50, 51
Job 42 38
Psalm 19 43
Psalm 45 43, 62n46
Psalm 55 3
Psalm 128 45
Proverbs 2 42, 63n52
Proverbs 3 34n48
Proverbs 5 17, 42
Proverbs 8 34n48
Proverbs 18 43
Proverbs 19 43, 59n16
Proverbs 21 59n16
Proverbs 25 59n16
Proverbs 27 59n16
Proverbs 30 36
Proverbs 31 17, 22–24, 32n30, 34n48, 45
Ecclesiastes 4 63n55
Song of Songs 2 42
Song of Songs 3 42
Song of Songs 4 42
Song of Songs 5 42
Song of Songs 6 42
Song of Songs 8 42
Isaiah 49 43
Isaiah 50 37, 57n2
Isaiah 54 42
Isaiah 56 32n35
Isaiah 61 43
Isaiah 62 44, 61n39
Jeremiah 2 42, 43
Jeremiah 3 37, 42, 44, 57n2
Jeremiah 7 61n39
Jeremiah 16 61n39
Jeremiah 25 61n39
Jeremiah 31 38
Jeremiah 33 61n39
Ezekiel 16 27, 42, 43, 44, 49–50
Ezekiel 18 38
Ezekiel 23 27, 44, 49–50
Daniel 6 38
Hosea 1–3 40, 44, 49, 70, 73n7, 73n8
Hosea 1 40
Hosea 2 27, 42, 44, 50, 59n15, 73n7
Hosea 3 40
Joel 1 42
Joel 2 43
Jonah 3 38
Jonah 4 38
Malachi 2 36, 41, 42, 56–57, 66

Greek Bible

Matthew 5 36–37, 54
Matthew 8 54
Matthew 9 44, 63n51
Matthew 19 9n14, 51, 64n73, 72n1
Matthew 22 44, 48, 51, 64n75
Matthew 25 44, 48
Matthew 27 31n21
Mark 2 44, 63n51
Mark 6 52
Mark 10 9n14, 17, 54
Mark 12 51, 64n75
Mark 15 31n21
Luke 5 44, 63n51
Luke 9 54
Luke 10 24
Luke 14 51, 54, 57n1
Luke 20 35n56, 51, 54
John 2 44
John 3 63n51
John 4 37
John 7 57n3
John 8 57n3, 63n56
John 19 31n21
Acts 5 43
Acts 8 32n35
Romans 1 19
Romans 3–8 38
1 Corinthians 5 59n16
1 Corinthians 7 15, 51, 56, 59n16, 60n28, 72n1

1 Corinthians 11 20, 21, 63n59
1 Corinthians 14 55
2 Corinthians 11 44
Galatians 3–4 38
Ephesians 5 9n14, 17, 30n16, 36, 41, 51, 54, 55–56, 61n34, 66, 69–70, 73n8
Ephesians 6 32n33
Colossians 3 17, 32n33, 55, 64n78, 65n79
1 Thessalonians 4 6
1 Peter 3 14, 17, 55, 58n7, 64n78
Revelation 2 70
Revelation 12 20
Revelation 19 44
Revelation 20 20
Revelation 21 44
Revelation 22 44

Deuterocanonical Books/ Apocrypha

Tobit 7 43, 63n50

Index of Authors and Subjects

abortion 8, 13, 21, 27, 29n7–8, 67
Afzal, S. 2–3, 8n1, 9n8, 9n10, 26, 30n14, 38, 71, 72, 73n5, 73n10
Alves, M. et al. 29n14
Aune, K. 68
Avisa Project 34n51
Ayers, D. J. 27
Azzoni, A. 41–42, 53, 60n24, 61n38

Bailey, W. 29n10
Barnes, R. 68
Barr, B. A. 9n11, 32n36, 35n55
Berlin, A. 5
Blyth, C. 8n2, 31n23, 35n55, 72, 73n7
Boyarin, D. 10n19
Brenner, A. 53
Brettler, M. Z. 5, 10n24
Brown, C. 9n11, 24, 35n58, 71
Brown, D. E. 9n13, 9n15, 16
Buchanan, P. 29n9
Buddhism 8n2
Burke, S. D. 32n35, 65n82
Byrd, A. 32n36, 35n55

Cappel, C. 68
Carden, M. 31n22
Carter, S. 64n78
Catholic(ism) 9n17, 11n29, 28n5, 29n10, 59n16
CBMW *see* Council for Biblical Manhood and Womanhood
celibacy *see* single life and/or celibacy
Chaudhry, A. 9n8, 65n80, 73n6
Christ *see* Jesus
clerical marriage 8, 11n29, 11n31
Clines, D. J. A. 29n11, 41, 61n36
Clough, M. 9n11, 35n58, 71, 72
Cobb, C. 9n18
Colgan, E. 8n2

complementarianism 12, 13, 14, 16, 19, 20, 21, 22–24, 28n3, 31n21, 31n24, 27, 32n29, 32n36, 33n37, 34n49, 34n53, 35n55, 45, 37, 46, 52, 53, 54, 55, 58n7, 66, 67, 68, 69
Council for Biblical Manhood and Womanhood (CBMW) 12, 13, 28n1, 28n4, 28n7, 29n8, 63n59, 66, 67
covenant 9n6, 26, 27, 32n31, 44, 51, 52, 63n52, 63n54, 64n67, 64n71, 67, 73n7

D'Angelo, M. R. 6, 31n21, 37, 44, 51, 59n13, 60n28, 64n72
Day, L. 64n66
Dead Sea Scrolls 57n3, 64n72
divorce 2, 7, 15, 18, 19, 24, 26–27, 34n53, 35n57, 36, 37, 40, 41, 45, 51, 52, 54, 56–57, 66, 67, 71, 72n1–2
Dobash, R. E. and R. Dobash 30n16, 35n58
Domoney-Lyttle, Z. 47
Du Mez, K. K. 10n27

Ebeling, J. R. 8n3
Edwards, K. B. 8n2, 10n26
Eisner, W. 5, 35n59
Elliot, E. 15, 27, 33n41, 34n50
Elliott, N. 30n16, 69
Everhart, R. 9n11, 24, 35n58, 71

Family Research Council (FRC) 12, 13, 16, 28n2, 28n4, 29n8, 32n31, 66, 67
Fea J. et al. 10n27

Index of Authors and Subjects

feminist/feminism 2, 9n8, 13, 14, 18, 19, 24, 25, 26, 27, 29n8, 29n13, 30n17, 32n27, 33n39, 33n41, 34n48, 34n52, 35n58, 67, 68
Ferguson, S. 9n9, 49
FRC *see* Family Research Council
Fussell, H. 29n8

Gafney, W. 60n25
Galambush, J. 64n66
Gevisser, M. 8, 11n31, 11n33, 19, 28n5
Gibson, E. L. 9n18
Glahn, S. 32n29
Gleig, A. 8n2
Gohmert, L. 39
Greenough, C. 30n15
Gretton-Dann, J. 33n37
Grudem, W. 13, 14, 15, 16, 17, 19–20, 21, 22, 27, 28n1, 28n7, 31n26, 33n44, 34n53, 56, 59n22, 61n41, 63n59
Guest, D. 31n22, 32n35, 53, 57, 65n82
Gur, H. R. 10n27

Haaken, J. 29n8
Harris, C. E. 29n14
Hobbs, V. 35n57, 68–69
Holben, L. R. 29n10, 31n25, 32n34, 58n8
homosexuality 13, 15, 16, 18–19, 29n7, 29n10, 14, 30n19, 31n25, 35n54, 52, 66, 67; *see also* LGBT(Q+); same-sex love/marriage
Hunter, A. 22, 32n27, 32n32, 34n48, 41, 42–43, 44–45, 53, 56, 57, 58n12, 59n14, 59n22, 60n27, 60n29, 60n31, 61n35, 61n37, 62n43, 63n50, 63n52, 64n70, 64n76

IICSA *see* Independent Inquiry into Child Sexual Abuse
incest 9n15, 19, 33n40, 39, 52, 58n6, 58n11
Independent Inquiry into Child Sexual Abuse (IICSA) 73n5
intermarriage 39, 45, 50–51, 52, 60n27, 64n70
Islam [check Muslim] 1, 8n2, 11n31, 11n32, 11n33, 30n14

Jesus 2, 8, 15, 24, 30n19, 31n21, 35n56, 36–37, 39, 44, 51, 53–54, 55, 56, 57n1, 57n3, 57n4, 63n56, 70

Johanna *see* Stiebert, J.
Johnson, A. J. 8n2, 35n58
Johnson, M. P. 35n58

Kahn-Harris, D. 8n4, 60n32, 65n82
Kalmanofsky, A. 8n2, 73n6
Kaziimba, S. S. 28n6
Kebaneilwe, M. 4
Keeya 35n54
Klopper, F. 3, 72
Knight, G. W. 23
Koepping, E. 8n2, 35n58, 66
Köstenberger, A. 2, 12, 15, 16, 18–19, 24, 26, 27, 30n19, 30n20, 34n53, 36, 37, 44, 52, 53, 56, 61n34, 63n52, 67, 69, 72n1
Kroeger, C. C. 64n77

Langenberg, A. 8n2
Lemos, T. 59n17
levirate marriage 45, 52, 58n6
Levitt, H. M. 73n6
LGBT(Q+) 11n33, 13, 18–19, 21, 27, 29n9, 29n14, 31n23, 32n35, 35n54, 52
Liew, T.-B. 60n22
Living in Love and Faith (LLF) 2, 7, 9n5, 12, 13, 26, 28n4, 29n12, 35n56, 61n34, 67, 69
LLF *see* Living in Love and Faith
Lynch, G. 24

Mackie, C. 51, 54, 55–56
Mankowski E. 29n8
Matthews, S. 9n18
McRae, P. 31n23
Morse, H. 33n37, 33n41, 43
Moscowitz, L. 4, 8
Muers, R. 65n80, 73n6
Murdock, G. P. 9n15

Newton, R. 65n81
Ng, Y. 62n44

Office for National Statistics (ONS) 7, 9n12, 35n58
ONS *see* Office for National Statistics
O'Rourke Boyle, M. 32n29
Ortlund, E. 42
Ortlund, R. C. 19, 24–25, 26, 30n17, 33n37, 34n52, 35n54
Ozanne Foundation 28n6, 58n10

Packer, J. 17
Parnass, S. 39
Patterson, D. 23, 32n28, 34n46
Paul (the Apostle) 8, 15, 20, 30n16, 51, 63n59, 65n81, 69
Paynter, H. 2, 9n7, 13, 14, 30n15, 35n58, 55, 56–57, 61n34, 65n81, 68, 72, 73n10
Perriello, P. 11n31
Pew Forum 34n53
Phillips, P. M. 10n26
pink line 8, 39
Piper, J. 13, 14, 15, 16–17, 19–20, 21, 22, 27, 30n18–19, 31n21, 31n26–27, 32n29–30, 33n44, 34n47, 34n53, 56, 63n59
polyamory 7, 8n4, 39, 60n32
Poythress, V. S. 23

Radford, L. 68
rape culture 3, 7, 8n2, 9n11, 37, 48, 49, 52, 70
Rashkover, R. 65n80, 73n6
Reinhartz, A. 29n13
Reissig, C. 29n8
Reaves, J. 9n18
Robinson, L. 47–48, 62n46
Rollens, S. 10n20

Sáenz-Badillo, A. 10n21
Saima *see* Afzal, S.
same-sex love/marriage 2, 7, 8, 8n4, 11n30–33, 13, 28n5–6, 39, 45, 53, 58n10, 61n40, 66; *see also* LGBT(Q+)
S.A.S. Rights 3, 8n1
Schäfer-Bossert, S. 10n22
Schmid, K. 57n3
Scholz, S. 62n43
Schreiner, T. R. 16, 20, 21
Schröter, J. 57n3
Scott, S. B. et al. 72n2
Sentamu, J. (Archbishop) 28n6
Septuagint (LXX) 9n17
Setel, T. D. 50, 64n66
Shelton, J. B. 68, 73n4
Sherwood, Y. 64n66
Shields, M. E. 64n66
Shiloh Project 3, 9n10
Shorter, R. 28n3, 31n24, 31n26, 66
single life and/or celibacy 15, 19, 30n19–20, 31n21, 51
Sivan, H. Z. 64n69

Sjoberg, L. 30n15
spiritual abuse 3, 9n12, 24, 52, 67, 68, 71, 72, 73n3
Stahl, A. 35n53
Starr, R. 67, 68
Stiebert, J. 1, 2–3, 5, 9n7–8, 9n10, 9n15, 29n14, 32n29, 33n40, 33n42, 35n56, 52, 58n11, 60n30, 63n60–61, 64n64, 68, 69, 70, 73n3, 73n5, 73n10
Stolakis, K. 11n33
Stone, K. 6, 10n22, 32n35
Stone, L. 58n7
supersessionism 5, 9n18, 10n20, 37

Taduggoronno, L. 11n31
Talmud 37
Tan, N. 3, 32n30, 34n48, 72, 73n7
Thatcher, A. 29n12, 33n38, 35n56
Thiede, B. 9n11, 33n41, 49, 60n32, 62n43, 63n49, 64n65
Tomalin, E. 9n12
Tombs, D. 31n21
Tong, M. A. 5, 67
trans(gender) *see* LGBT(Q+)
translation 6–7, 10n22–23, 16, 17, 21, 22, 30n17, 31n27, 32n35, 33n43, 36, 40, 41, 43, 47, 49, 55, 56, 59n14, 59n16, 61n40–41, 62n42–43, 63n54, 63n62, 64n65, 64n70, 65n80
Trible, P. 31n27, 33n39, 42, 62n41
Tucker, R. 68, 71

Vanden Eykel, E. 9n18, 10n20
van Dijk-Hemmes, F. 64n66
van Klinken, A. 11n31, 30n14, 31n22, 32n35, 35n54, 72
virgin/ity 15, 18, 28, 31n21, 47, 48, 49, 59n16–17, 64n63

Ware, K. N. 73n6
Warren, M. 10n20, 37, 73n9
wedding 4, 7, 10n28, 28n6, 40, 41, 42, 43–44, 47–48, 50, 56, 61n39–40, 63n53
Weems, R. 2, 64n66
Welby, J. (Archbishop) 28n6
West, G. 4
Westenberg, L. 68
World Health Organisation (WHO) 7

Young, S. 70

For Product Safety Concerns and Information please contact our EU representative GPSR@taylorandfrancis.com
Taylor & Francis Verlag GmbH, Kaufingerstraße 24, 80331 München, Germany

www.ingramcontent.com/pod-product-compliance
Lightning Source LLC
Chambersburg PA
CBHW051759230426
43670CB00012B/2354